Looking Out onto Our World

Explorations of Power, Dogma, and
a World Deserving Contemplation

Copyright © 2020 by T. P. Graf

All rights reserved.
No portion of this book may be reproduced
in any form without permission from the author,
except as permitted by U.S. copyright law.

ISBN 978-1-7352332-6-0

amazon.com/author/tpgraf
TP Graf on Facebook
tpgraf@pm.me

For all on a journey from
narrow ideology and dogma
to abundant love and compassion.

A note to the reader

Throughout these pages, there are intentional references
to "man" and "men" as representative of the patriarchal
systems that have dominated human history; these
are not meant to be read as gender-neutral terms.

Writings of T.P. Graf

As the Daisies Bloom - A Novel

PenCraft Awards - 2020 First Place, Cultural Fiction
Book Excellence Awards - 2021 Finalist, Friendship
Chanticleer IBA, 2020 First Place, Somerset Book Awards

A beautiful telling of life's trials and tribulations, always overcome by the love of family and of something greater than oneself. - Reader's Favorite

Enchanting as it is charming ... intimately and poetically told ... like a well-written symphony - Literary Titan

A powerfully written character-led novel; stark and unsettling but often funny too. Highly recommended! - A 'Wishing Shelf' Book Review

August Kibler's Stories for Tyler
Voices of Context from Eden to Patmos
(Companion to As the Daisies Bloom)

Firebird Award - 2021 Winner, Christian Poetry
American Book Awards - 2021 Finalist, Religious Poetry
Royal Dragonfly, 2021 Honorable Mention, Religion/Spirituality

A compelling and thought-provoking study of the bible and Christian history. The writing style is almost angelic! It's the sort of book you want to discuss; that stays with you for a long, long time.
- A 'Wishing Shelf' Book Review

Graf has crafted a masterful work of modern literature that takes on some very complex topics...in a format that any reader can engage with and glean wisdom from ... entertaining ... highly recommend.
- Reader's Favorite

The book offers fresh ideas ... absorbing ... thought-provoking and evokes a positive emotional connotation. - Literary Titan

Roots, Branches and Buzz Saws
More Stories of August Kibler

"Celebrate who you are, even if it is quietly...". That is what this book is, a celebration of August's life and a reminder to the reader to celebrate their life, who they are. - Literary Titan

This book is a perfect example of how each life is valuable and is a story to tell...important ... impactful ... perfect slice-of-life novel
- Readers' Favorite

Insightful, powerful, a story of life and how it's changed by so many tiny happenings. Highly recommended! - A 'Wishing Shelf' Book Review

Looking Out onto Our World
Explorations of Power, Dogma and a World Deserving of Contemplation

Insightful, intelligent; the sort of poetry that will stay with you for a long time. Highly recommended. - A 'Wishing Shelf' Book Review

Alive with sensory experience...refusing standard conventions of storytelling...confident...each word in each verse deliberate ... arranged for maximum impact...ripping and compelling ... will engage even the most reluctant poetry reader. - Literary Titan

Introspective ... thoughtful and fascinating a realistic observation of life's journey ... with an eye towards hope and celebration ... full of emotive and intelligent wordplay ... highly recommended ... a great pick me up and talking point to share with others.
- Reader's Favorite

The Life and Stories of Jaime Cruz (Trilogy)

Chanticleer IBA, 2021 Finalist, Laramie Book Awards:
TP Graf for a Series - Americana Western Fiction
International Impact Book Awards, Winner, TP Graf - Author for a Series
Chanticleer IBA, 2022 Finalist - Book Series Award

Tumbleweed and Dreams (Book One)
From the Series - The Life and Stories of Jaime Cruz

Firebird Award - 2021 Winner, Book in a Series

Firebird Award - 2021 Winner, Multicultural Fiction
American Fiction Awards - 2021 Finalist, Multicultural Fiction
Hollywood Book Festival - 2021 Honorable Mention, General Fiction
Book Excellence Awards - 2023 Finalist, Multicultural Fiction

Graf manages to keep readers enthralled with Jaime's day-to-day experiences chapter after chapter ... a beautifully penned tale of self-discovery and a strong main character who stands out in a crowd.
- Literary Titan

A gripping story filled with colorful and often captivating characters.
- A 'Wishing Shelf' Book Review

An immersive journey of self-discovery and a sense of home ... you find yourself invested in the lives of the people and the friendships that are made. - Readers' Favorite

Night Air Descending (Book Two)
From the Series - The Life and Stories of Jaime Cruz

A cleverly-crafted, character-led family drama set in Texas. I got so immersed in it, I started to feel like one of the family too!
- A 'Wishing Shelf' Book Review

Whether you're in the mood for a slice-of-life drama or a study of eclectic characters, Night Air Descending by T.P. Graf is a memorable read.
- Readers' Favorite

This is a beautifully written book that has a grounded and authentic feel so much that it feels like we are reading someone's diary ... heartwarming ... [with a] distinct literary aesthetic. - Literary Titan

Seeds in the Desert Wind (Book Three)
From the Series - The Life and Stories of Jaime Cruz

Every quirk, every nuance, and each daily challenge make this story relatable and enjoyable...a book that wraps around you like your favorite blanket and touches your heart in a unique way. - Literary Titan

Graf again delivers interesting, full-bodied characters that we can relate to and want to follow through to their conclusions...

a story that will entertain and move you. - Readers' Favorite

A powerful, often thought-provoking end to this excellent trilogy. Highly recommended. - A 'Wishing Shelf' Book Review

A Cowgirl's Stories
Companion to The Life and Stories of Jaime Cruz Trilogy

Sallie is such a special character ... I adore that readers do not necessarily know where Sallie will take us next. The unpredictability of her tales is endearing in the best possible way. - Literary Titan

You'll certainly be hooked on the attitude and atmosphere of the world so lovingly crafted. - Readers' Favorite

*A richly textured and often humorous story of a life growing up in Texas ... full of revelations and insights into a totally different world.
- The 'Wishing Shelf' Book Review*

Days in the Desert
Food for Body and Soul

Delicious and nutritious! - Reader Review

Fort Davis, TX, 2001–2012

For the Cause	1
Dusk at Mano Prieto Mountains	3
Treaty of Unending War	6
Grace to Ponder	8
For Three Prophets	9
Naked Soul	17
Let's Get It On	18
$100,000,000	20
Elegy to Marthella Rupp Graf (1926–2006)	21
Swiss@Heart	22
The Therapist & The Monk	23
Body and Soul	25
Original Confusion	26
Journeymen and Doublewides	27
Grama	29
Epiphany and the Church of God—Amtrak	30
Planned to Death	32
The Wrong of Rights	35
Mission of Dignity	37
Thirty-one Haiku	39
Mr. Corporation	45
Left, Right, and Center	47
God in a Box	49
Flip the Switch	50
Mascot	51
The Path	52
State of Confusion	53
American Credo	55
Angels of Our Nature	58
Aperture to the World	59

The Ant and Her Man	60
End-times Schizophrenia	61
On a Line from Daniel Koh	62
Daydream	63
The Amish and the Church of God–Amtrak	66
The Boys and Ego—Return on Investment (ROI)	69
Forgive My Lack of Originality	70
Ideal's Reality	70
Answerman	71
Elegy to Johnny Graf (1924–1993)	72
Odd Fits	75
Fragments of Our Myth	75
u-a-p	76
Lotto Fever	76
Crimson Seas	77
Oh, Sophia	80
Heavenly Drone	80
Credo in Unum Deum	81
Summation	84
The Ends	85
Night Benediction	85
Glittering Diamonds	86
Told-ya-so	87
Just Desserts	87
We, the People	88
Clingers	88
Hell as Concept	89
Disturbing Definitions	90
The Gospel According to Huck Finn	91
Zero Sum Game	94
Closure of Pain	94

Grief's Work 94
The Walk 95
Contemplation's Fruit 96
Computation 97
My Moodiness 98
Love in Question 99
Tyranny 99
Claims 100
Elegy to Laura (Viator) Gardener (1928–2012) 101
Purchased Votes 102
Trinity as Concept 103
What May Be 105
Journey 106
Church as Concept 107
Elegy to Gary Oyer (1956–1975) 108
Vision Without Blinders 108
In all Deference to Jefferson 109
Quarrelsome 109
What We Instill 110
Red and Blue 111
Point of Our Play 112
Digging 113
Checks and Balances 113
None of the Above 114
Dull Perception 115

Mount Dora, FL, 2013–2015

On a line from Barbara Douglas 116
Bound 117
Violence in the Night 118
Presumption 119

Turn Our Eyes from Ourselves 120
Culpability..122
A Prophet's Pondering Way 122
Image...123
Intertwined...124
For Desmond Tutu 125
Shaken and Stirred 126
Snippet..127
Gradualism...128
Momma Said..130
A Stand for Love of Country 133
Fantasism..134
What Lives Become 135
In Flight..136
Posing Questions...140
Mistaken Identity 142
A Brief Exchange...142
Replica Masses...143
Movings..145
Is It I?..145
Libera Shuffle...146
Checklist Traveler 148
Final Heartbeat 149
Focus 150
Cussin' Work 150
Pseudonym's Story 151
USA Today 152
Uber Austin 152

Blanco, TX and Lake Diane MI, 2016–2019

Party of the RPC and the 2016 Election Cycle.................153

Faulty Foundations	155
New Day	157
The Thriller	159
Party Animals	160
Rabid Passion	161
Care	161
Mercy	161
On a Line by Raimond Gaita	162
Moving to the Edge	163
No Denial	165
Baggage-Burden	166
Francis in Washington	167
Raspberries from My Garden	169
Boiling Pot	170
On Lines by Khalifa Al-Khadr	171
General Nonsense	173
Charity	174
More Evil Dreams of Night	175
Media Storm	177
The Demagogue	178
The Refugee	178
Tick-tock	180
Mercy's Accounting	181
Thoughts on a New Economy	182
Off the Pavement	187
Easter 2017	188
Thoughts on a June Morning	189
Holding Hands with Amos	190
Draft Horse Journal	193
Elegy to Bob Huffaker (1936–2018)	196
Betrayal	197

Tweet-tweet 198
Mr. Lee in Particular 198
Intervention Obsession 200
Sainthood for the Warmonger 201
The Time of Old Dogs and the Old Master 202
Amish Guard Dogs 204

Beech Mountain, NC, December 2019–

The New Year, 2020 206
The Memo 208
The States of Mind and Soul 213
Elegy to Jack Corwin Graf (1947–2020) 215
The Chasm 217
Finding Joy Beyond the Noise 218
The Inspiration of Dickens 221
April 2020 224
Dark Hour of the Soul 226

In Closing

A Canticle for Peace 228

Fort Davis, TX, 2001–2012

For the Cause
(Reflecting on the "Live Earth" concerts, summer 2007)

With vehement passion,
    we stand in anger's dread to stop the nuclear power
that generates the life support system
    our clutching grip on life demands.
No thrift, no simplified life required.

(Just carry the sign, comrade.)

While Al Qaeda, in bidding war,
whose weapons of fear and hate
predate recorded history,
    drives us
    in fear's response
to send off in constant vigilance the B-52 and its
thermo-destructive superiority and ultimate suppression.
    We press on with duty to country.

(Support the troops, patriot.)

    At the same time, the PC mindful,
whose checkbooks grew fatter but from
the Capitalist unfettered accumulation of all,
write a check to some environmental cause
    as the oblation for so many
first-class upgrades in the jet-stream.
And the stadium parking lot packs,
with rows of personal oversized transport
with their global warming bumper-stickers
to hear the mega-watt juice of another rock concert,
    to "save the planet"

    from the millions
    like themselves.

(Buy a carbon offset, progressive.)

Our causes perpetuate so much use of resource
    (we hold as detestable),
while our grip holds secure to the toys of our comfort.
Darkness and silence offer more light than fear,
but fear's grip demands noise, activity, protest.

(Vote the party back into power, citizen.)

    Come stillness.
Unplug us from the strident media and
antagonistic discourse of so many barbarian zealots.
Let the march stop with our rightful distrust
of information without wisdom.
    Speak to us,
    Quiet Spirit,
through the whispering details
of nature's re-creation around us.
Save us from the saviors of so many self-serving causes.
    And bring us, wholly,
    to gentle reason
    and humble peace within.

(Love all, my daughter, my son.)

Dusk at Mano Prieto Mountains
(Reflecting on the "dark hand" mountains surrounding home,
autumn 2007)

We sit in silence following the silence of Compline,
    where the chapel,
        already in shadow,
looks out to the dark-hand mountain in the east—
still illuminated by the sun drifting to other lands.
It is easy to see the eternity of space on this cloudless day.
The desert sky by day—by night—contains within itself
    a vastness that makes
the silhouette of the native oak to its place,
    seem a humble offering indeed.
It stands bent from the west winds;
its life in the rock on the ridge
of the western finger of the dark hand
is a reminder to the transplanted creature,
that life here is not easy but
finds its own shape and contentment.
    Why care for this place?
    Why care for any place?

The sounds between day and night here
echo the distant truck and the soft splash of the fountain.
As night descends, other sounds echo within.
    The cactus wren,
now pronouncing her benediction,
flies to her precarious nest atop the cholla;
beneath the bramble of mesquite and tumbleweed
broods the covey of quail.
Soon the coyot's will offer their night song
to the otherwise hushed world living
in the respectful peace of monk's silence.

Perhaps there is no God,

as some believe.
If they are right, then life here has only one chance
of the evolving creature showing that its
intelligence can live on this celestial island
with a greater awareness of purpose
than the bat circling in the twilight
beginning his nightlong work.
    A simple fate,
        though yet unrealized.
It must have awareness of the earth and water,
as the piñon has in its contented spring growth.
The awareness must take in the galaxy
that gives the night grand splendor
that the assembly line of filaments at
great cost can only mock in cheap imitation.

Perhaps there is a God, as some believe—
    as I believe. If we are right,
how can we love God and hate creation?
Our faith, an assurance of things hoped for,
is a hope I live because of creation—
    not in spite of it.
It is in great shifts of nature's mysterious violence
    that new life emerges.
It is in peaceful balance that new life flourishes.
The human mind labors greatly on
    controlling,
    perpetrating,
    perpetuating
the violence of evil. It builds great cities
by choking lands for water;
robbing soil for parking lots filled with its assembled
scraps of metal and plastic. Our lots lay cast with people
standing in the ubiquitous burg of the gated consumer.

The creature burns and destroys in wars for right
and purpose with a purposefulness that brings
    wealth to few and
    misery to many.
The creature, with the great mind to create,
has squandered his call to new life
flourishing in the peaceful balance.
The pace set by man
    (bearing the burden of *his* own history of domination)
is not finished in his nature. Man
must make more—by day, by night.
More of what the earth cannot give except by its depletion.
More of its breath turned to toxic gas.
More for more's sake—needed or not, so long as
    profit is served and
    plunder divided.
Yet the autumn finds its stillness.
The swallow, who darts playfully in the sunlit days,
finds shelter in the eve inside her mud-packed hut.
The white-tailed buck moves from his day-long rest.

Come, believer and atheist,
to the peace lost to minds who race from
    peaceableness to destruction.
Let nature's violence rule the created world.
Let nature's peace bring the creature of the dark hand with
his brothers and sisters to a place of peace where life
flourishes—just as contented
    mongrel dogs find safe sleep
    on the coolness of concrete
    just inside the screen door.

Treaty of Unending War
(Reflecting on the latest news reports of drone attacks killing civilians in Pakistan, spring 2011)

Predatory drones drone on night and day.
Any vestige of dignity long removed.
    Eden obliterated by fire for profit.
From a windowless existence, a human drone
in the Nevada desert with joystick and computer
aims death, obeying an order that says,
    "Kill here."
Connected by satellites of hate, two deserts press on
in evil pursuit of a peace defined as the end of the other.
The gates of hell, ever burning, banish us once again
from the Garden, perfect in its complex microcosm.
Our acts, now trillions upon trillions spent
    (seems inconceivable),
press on from war room to boardroom.
Ripping sinew from flesh as if satiating the sacred
hunger of some great carrion feeder.
    Yet, it is only smallness that is fed.
    Bidding of the money changers.
    Pride of the politician.
Humility lost in the power, and the grace of Christ
cast deep in murky shadows
beyond the pools of blood and stench.
Invasions of "peace-making," which permeates
an ever-charring landscape of debris and retribution
    with its exhausted breath.
Now, as the dead waters flow into the ancient seabeds,
so the dim-witted madmen under their flags
pour injustice on ancient cultures and lands.
    Condescension, their self-made right—
    lost to human obligation.

Scatter the generals, the politicians, and

gather the peaceable, lest justice be denied in perpetuity.
Sow the great seeds of compassion and love.
Bind up the tortured body and soul of the victim—
    soldier and civilian.
Loosen the cords of greed for the simple thrift
of a good earth's free gifts.
    Awaken to the life of grace perfected,
    which needs no stars and stripes or
    patriotic tune to find its worth.

Grace to Ponder
(Reflecting on the essay, *Prerequisite to Dignity of Labor,* by Simone Weil (1909–1943))

Sound bites offer very little of worth to chew on.
To understand the evil of an economy,
    no sound bite will do.
One might as well go gathering
eggs in the cuckoo clock
as look for wisdom in the fragmentary pretexts of
    narrow thought
    offered in the twenty-four/seven cable news cycle.
The world condensed to
    the overstated,
    the understated,
but never the wholly stated.

Time is better spent transfixed, pondering sunlight's blessed
gifts of pasture and vineyard and fruit tree.
    Light ethereal,
    warming us,
    feeding us,
    but never possessed by us.
For the greatest gifts to humanity
remain the free gifts of creation
that graced the earth eons before the cheapness
of slogan and party line demanded our allegiance—
    belittling our worth.
Ponder the renewal of the glorious re-creation
when the last homo sapiens of hate have finally destroyed
    all that was inconceivable—
    all that was theirs
    to treasure and
    not destroy,
including themselves and their children's children.

For Three Prophets

I. Wendell Berry (1934–)
(Berry quotations in order of occurrence: 1) excerpt from the poem *My Great-Grandfather's Slaves* from *Collected Poems*; 2) excerpt from a poem on hope from *Leavings*; 3) excerpt from the essay, *The Purpose of a Coherent Community*, from *The Way of Ignorance*; 4) excerpt from the poem, *I Dream of a Quiet Man* from the collection, *Given*)

Set apart by holistic vision,
you wander among the Kentucky hills of your birth.
Seeing the scars we all bear in our exploitation, yet
    grace ever-present in your thoughts.
    Eyes opened in humility to the painful legacy
of your kind owning the flesh of another kind.
Uneasy in the distance still between race and creed.

("I know that freedom can only be given, and it is the gift to the giver from the one who receives.")

You, who taught us to see the purchased power and its evils:
    greed, fear,
    tyranny, war,
    destruction,
veiled behind a false diplomacy and empty patriotism
that loves control and holds in contempt
    all things small and free.
Pushing against progress as defined by profit only,
you bear a burden not unlike the carpenter of Galilee
who called us to love the enemy
    about and within.

("No place at last is better than the world. The world is no better than its places. Its places are at last no better than their people while their people continue in them. When the people make dark the light within them, the world darkens.")

Tol and Jayber and Hannah; Andy, Art, and Old Jack;
Burley and Elton and Mary; through your beloved, imagined
Port William, we are moved to a vision
of our imperfect lives perfected by
    good work,
    care, thrift,
    patience, grace.
Women and men, wholly part of your mind, given over to a
reverence for our failings and foibles, reminding us that
laughter, tears, birth, and death are the many milestones
enriching us along the *Way of Ignorance*.

("There is no escape from the issue of context, and if we think
of modern life in terms of context, we are going to find it
abounding in inconsistencies and moral discomforts that we
have taught ourselves not to feel.")

Like all peacemakers, you madden
    the selfish,
    the self-serving,
    the self-righteous.
Like all peacemakers, you are praised in overly simple
platitudes by the politician whose legacy of evil stands
in sharp relief against your Sabbath heart.
Like all peacemakers, you see the blessed beauty
    of fleeting things,
    so temporal in their days,
    so eternal in their wonder, freely given over to being.

("I dream of a quiet man who explains nothing and defends
nothing, but only knows where the rarest wildflowers are
blooming and who goes, and finds that he is smiling not by
his own will.")

The timbered choir of Kentucky stands
in quiet respect to the contrarian

> who wanders about its ancient glory,
> > knowing that his flesh carries the atoms
>
> of its long history and that its beauty
> rests in comfortable silence in a mind that nurtures
> > birdsong and Godsong
>
> as sacred Easter gifts of our destiny.

II. Martin Luther King, Jr. (1929–1968)

(Quotations from *Beyond Vietnam: A Time to Break Silence,* a sermon at the Riverside Church delivered by Martin Luther King Jr. on April 4, 1967)

Amid the caricature of a dream made small
to fit the visionless of humanity,
> you are recast from prophet to
> celebrity hero,
> a tourist attraction
> for those on the mall

who need the nonthreatening presence of silent stone.
We play bits of "I have a dream" over and over,
while lost to the archives, except to those who seek the truth
or stumble haphazardly upon it, lies "Beyond Vietnam."
Still bearing witness to a truth the lords
of power must hide from.
But beneath words, so damning they could only be spoken
> out of love,

the wars of ignorance—the poison of Truman,
drunk in the sacramental chalice of democracy's defenders:
> Eisenhower,
> Kennedy,
> Johnson,
> Nixon—

rage on still with this generation's
ever-growing list of hollow-shelled strident defenders.

("Rationalizations and the incessant search for scapegoats are the psychological cataracts that blind us to our sins. But the day has passed for superficial patriotism. He who lives with untruth lives in spiritual slavery.")

Your divinely colored face was more than
the defenders of separation could bear,
for you bore within your eyes the reflection
of love, staring back where hate should have been,
as it was when their reflection was cast upon
    their own mirrored souls.
You stirred the conscience against the three great evils.
    Poverty for its indifference to suffering;
    racism for its denial of humanity;
    militarism for its cowardly profits
    and wonted destruction.
Binding us up, you walked with the humility and courage
of one who cannot know defeat, save from
    not making the walk.
Binding us up, you cried out for compassion
for all—enemy and stranger.
Binding us up, you carried us to our freedom, for only in
    knowing the truth can we be free.

("Could it be that they do not know that the Good News was meant for all men, for communists and capitalists, for their children and ours, for black and white, for revolutionary and conservative. Have they forgotten that my ministry is in obedience to the One who loved His enemies so fully that he died for them?")

Conformist thought, which patronized the poor, moved
    with such expediency,
every victory for "rights" produced
    an equal measure of wrongs
    as the ghetto

   replaced the taskmaster
as the oppressor of a centuries-oppressed people.
Voiced as radical ways, your compassion for the destruction
of the villages and the families of a brown-skinned people
  of our broken promise of freedom,
stood in near-singular expression as the hope for
   their redemption
   and ours as a nation.
Our deadly arrogance you stood against with more courage
than the sword can ever falsely endow upon its bearer.

("There's something strangely inconsistent about a nation
and a press that will praise you when you say, 'Be non-violent toward Jim Clark,' but will curse and damn you when you say, 'Be non-violent toward little brown Vietnamese children.'")

Never comfortable in assuming a place assigned to you
by the reckoning of a race who could not conceive
  of an equality for all,
you led all those who inherently knew their place was defined
by a just God and not by a failed humanity,
to know their dignity as divinely endowed.
From the mountaintop of justice,
you poured down the mighty waters
  of peace and love.
As though carrying the weight of a worn and weary nation,
you moved us to know
   there is no perfection where there is no Gospel;
   there is no perfection where hate
   makes its ethical compromises in fire and fear.

("We have been repeatedly faced with a cruel irony of watching Negro and white boys on TV screens as they kill

and die together for a nation that has been unable to seat
them together in the same school room.")

Still, under the curse of war, your ear
    to the broken cries of all
remains our prophetic call to walk the path
    of freedom and truth;
our prophetic call to walk in humility and justice
    on the Jericho road of life.

III. Simone Weil (1909–1943)
(Weil quotations in order of occurrence: 1) excerpt from the essay *Human Personality*, from *Simone Weil-An Anthology*; 2) excerpt from *Gravity and Grace*; 3) excerpt from *Draft for a Statement of Human Obligations*, from *Selected Essays, 1934-1943: Historical, Political and Moral Writings*)

You might have known a longer,
    less struggle-filled life
had you known the like mind of Berry,
a gentle shepherd for those who struggle with conscience,
but you came into a world of
    communism,
    fascism,
    capitalism,
all staking a claim for pride and progress while suffering
abounded in your beloved France.
With the uneasy reckoning of your own privileged past,
you threw yourself into a rationed way of life
that finally defeated your weak body,
    though never your mind.
A testimony to dignity, worth, responsibility,
your words compel us to renounce the myths and monsters
of absolutism and to adopt an active conversation
on context, relations, and limits.

("Clearly, a political party busily seeking, or maintaining itself in power can discern nothing in these cries [against evil] except a noise...It can never be capable of the tender and sensitive attention which is needed to understand its meaning.")

Baptism of a Spirit you did not seek and
    the waters to which you could not assent
brought you, in mystic contradiction and
clarity, to a place where the feared "I" and
even more greatly feared "we" could be
    led from God by a rousing Nazi chorus—
    so magnetized are we to pomp and power.
Yet the "I" you were
found a God for which love was its great confirmation
and a God you refused to find in an
    anthropomorphism to suit "I's" fancy.

("I am other than what I imagine. To know this is forgiveness.")

From the factory floor and the tents
    of the Spanish Civil War, you consumed little,
yet you always fed your insatiable hunger of dignity
    for the laborer,
    for the soldier,
    for the suffering.
Their pain was your pain, and through it you moved
to find the consolation of healing brought by God,
    despite the flawed earthly agents of that divine will.
Your small, imperfect hands sealed a vision
for common humanity in an uncommon mind
of grace—embracing the gifts
    of sun and
    season and soil
as the inerrant teachers of our senses.

("Any place where the needs of human beings are satisfied
can be recognized by the fact that there is a flowering of
fraternity, joy, beauty, and happiness.")

Outside the steeple's walls, you remained
    in measured contemplation
of an embrace of God no apostasy could rouse;
no episcopate could render sure. You, the outside voice,
whose revelations bespoke the inside workings
    of justice and love.

Naked Soul

Young and naked in the Garden,
the paradigm is set as the utopia
    of "free market" consumerism
instills the eternal hunger for more.
From the fruit of its deceit,
    an assurance is provided
of perfection within reach, which is a mirage,
while the dusty messenger crawls off
for another day's lies to come.
We, the children of Eve, scoff at the madness
    of the Holy Fool,
beside which all wisdom of the world is left wanting,
as we consume the food of our exile.

The love of God, with its claim on humanity,
follows the exiles with a heart always toward pardon,
    where pardon may be cast away
    as cheap—so easily are we fooled
    by all that glitters.
We remain blind to compassion, even when it cries
divine forgiveness in its bloody submission
    to our hate and fear.

The soul, nailed to the agony of the cross,
awaits its hopeful consummation
    of grace revealed,
    of shame removed,
    of love unfettered.
And so hope returns as the young and naked
    stand as one again, in greater humility,
before the first dawn of creation's perfect light.

Let's Get It On

For all the moralizing we do about intimate
relations, do we really think the heavenly
hosts are voyeuristically transfixed on the
now constant climax of the several hundred
thousand at any given time (simple mathematical
probabilities of the libido of four billion capable
adults assumed), as the TV preacher would
have us believe? Or does age at least give way
to Ms. Sayers' wise words of
    "joyless passion" as "sin"
and her observation, as
    "I totter nearer towards the tomb,
    I find that I care less and less,
    who goes to bed with whom."

Mr. Gaye got it closer to the truth, even for the
congregants of the Church of Carnal Judgement.
    C'mon, baby.
    Do you know the meaning?
    I've been sanctified.
    Let's get it on!
Our shame is our selfishness and disregard for
the sanctity of the other. There is no shame in
naked flesh's sweet embrace with another,
all curled up together as one, just as the first man
and woman in the Garden in all their
Holy Innocence and procreational necessity.
    Adam and Eve,
    Aaban and Steve,
    Rivka and Veve
    (perfect love casts out fear),
each knit together in the Sacred
womb in its own unique and blessed
personhood, in coupled pairings,

come together in a glory that must
clearly deem Heaven's solemn role,
>   *Ubi caritas et amor,*
>   *Deus ibi est.*
>   *Exultemus!*

$100,000,000
(A reflection on Virgin Galactic's October 2011 test launch for its planned space tourism industry)

    With tax-funded giddy glee,
Spaceport America in the New Mexico desert,
awaits five hundred paid-up patrons of the
    galactically greedy
for the launch of WhiteKnight
    (white power still prevails),
with its $200,000 joy ride in space.
The champions of
    galactic tourism,
    alternative fuels, and
    carbon offsets
would do well to offset their own carbon footprint
by actually not burning carbon and
keeping their feet grounded on the only Earth we've got.
Icy crystals on a Jupiter moon are not going to water
the drought-stricken lands of the horn of Africa—neither shall
a five-minute weightless ride in space,
    the promised highlight of the ride.
Turning crops into rocket fuel does not feed the starving.
Flying carbon composites still means energy burned
    for the latest human technological folly.
Oh, great consumer of the orbit,
    bid you hammer your rockets into plowshares;
    bid you share your wealth with the small organic
farmer and rancher and with the local shopkeeper;
    bid you stop casting your treasure to the swine herd
    of human waste and destruction.

Elegy to Marthella Rupp Graf (1926–2006)

Death by the medical industrial complex,
    protracted in suffering,
we fight with stubborn determinism
    that last great heroic struggle,
but such a resistance is as much blind obedience
to strangers masked behind unending cures and
our own simple denial of the reality—
    death comes to us all.
Embracing, curiously and conversationally,
    that great inevitability
that can be, and indeed should be, the grace perfected
that we pass along to all we love as the
welcoming understanding
of a life fully and wondrously lived and loved,
now come to its end, and for the fellowship
    of its final rest in peace.
For this gift, which you bestowed, we give you thanks.

Swiss@Heart

Perhaps it is some inexplicable genetic predisposition
    of the Graf, Schudel, Winzeler,
    Seiler, Kübler, Merillat,
    Beck, Gearig, and König
ancestors of mine who left
    Cantons Schaffhausen, Basel, and Bern
to spend their remaining days in Fulton County, Ohio,
that draws me back to their
    pulled-up roots of the 1800s.
Perhaps it is two hundred fifty years of peace,
when my own country has known two hundred fifty
    years of war.
Perhaps it is green grass, snowcapped mountains,
    crystal-clear streams.
Perhaps it is the tolerance for language, dialect, and culture.
Perhaps it is the egalitarian nature of the place.
Perhaps it is the small farms, well-cared-for animals,
    built-to-last buildings, tidy places.
Or perhaps I just have
    a Swiss heart for *what can be*
instead of the American heart of *what must be*.

The Therapist & The Monk

Eager in their pride to affix their own importance
to our social construct, the therapists of
Hollywood screens perpetually compel us,
    "Let it all out!"
And so our generations have complied. The
young husband escalates a needless argument
over the thermostat into a rage that ends with,
    "Fuck you!"
a sentiment expressing the full contempt of
unchecked anger. The man, in midlife crisis,
now doubtful of his own assurance of success, held in
trust to date by an American dream, and trapped in
a job devoid of dignity, curses whatever group of
"them" his mind can conjure.
    "Goddamn Mexicans!"
    "Goddamn Muslims!"
    "Goddamn faggots!"
Any group will do, so long as blame falls with those
unworthy of his flag. Watching the TV couple
kiss, the old man, sucking oxygen, his only link
to life after too many years sucking tobacco tar
into his lungs, removes the mask
just long enough to say,
    "I can't stand to see two niggers kiss."

They do not know the monastery wisdom that
guides the monk and all his thoughts (his
management of truth). For the silent voice informs
his mind of the grace essential to his day—
words not held for meek consideration for another
    fester the destruction of this world.

In his cycle of silence, he enters the chapel in
the long robes of his brothers in contemplation

to repeat the millennia-old prayers of the Psalms.
Expressed, in humble trust, are his own
anger, loathing, fears, and hates, leading him
to the greater measure of their divine
    grace,
    peace,
    love.
Holding to these in renewed trust, he makes his final
deep and reverent bow to the sacramental presence,
walking back into his silent world and into the
abyss of mysterious darkness
    made light by love.

Body and Soul

After the long day of cooking, serving
and cleaning for the crowd, I call it an
early night, only to find my bed uneasy
with my early presence. It tosses me back
and forth as the old bones (convinced that my
hearing is gone, as well as my good sense)
scream their report of the day.
    "Feet in pain!
    Legs in Pain!
    Back in pain!
    Hands, arms, and neck in pain!"
The body having finished its report, the soul
only smiles and retorts its eternal truth,
    "Soul alive and well!"
And so it is, the old body comes to rest.

Original Confusion

    Holiness and perfect charity
breathed into our dust to bring us life,
though sadly, my suspicions too confirmed,
the doctors of the Church wrote other rules.
    Augustine on a grumpy day
set forth procreation's concupiscence failings,
confirmed for all descendants of that first conjugated love.
    Luther and Calvin,
sure of innocence lost forever, did little to sway the way.
Aquinas seemed to want to steer the mighty ship
    of the evil-endowed back toward
    its more grace-filled course,
but the winds of guilt and fear and shame pushed ever-on.
    Before original sin
(which in its execution is usually anything but),
the Creator spoke another word—
    less heavy than the lords of doctrine and creed,
    more worthy of Love's pure image as conceived.
Behold, all is good. We, in our original innocence,
must make our choice,
but for this choice, we also must observe—
    with silence refused, in favor of the noise,
    how can Love's discernment guide our way?

Journeymen and Doublewides
(A reflection on two righteous journeymen, Johannes Krasnenko
and Patrick Kunkel, working in Murten, Switzerland, October 2011)

    Caring for the Rathaus Murten,
two righteous journeymen of Carpenters and Slaters
put their skills to task on six hundred years
of standing wood and stone.
    With eight buttons on the waistcoat
    for the hours worked each day and
six buttons for the six working days each week,
two men, in black corduroy, among a thousand others,
have left their homes with less money in their pocket
    then would buy a stein and sausage.
They will return home in three years and one day
    with the same or less.
For eight hundred years, these tradesmen
have been "on the waltz," honoring skill,
thrift, a day's good work; ever dependent on others
    for food,
    a ride, a place to rest, and
    a full day's work.
Not staying too long, so as not to become dependent
    on the place,
they know they must move on when the neighbors kiss them
    and the dogs no longer bark.
Their years pass with time given freely when others demand
the expected wages logged by clocks of time.

    In sharp relief, across the pond,
the journey is of another kind—the ubiquitous double-wide
headed for the cluttered countryside
    in its growing shoddiness and disregard.
    A house that depreciates
in equal measure to the vehicles parked
in the drive, ensuring a poverty that robs us of our worth.

The Righteous Journeyman looks on with pity at a building
that is so predestined in its fate.
> Such temporal use is beyond his comprehension.

His affection is for that which is constructed
> in love with a beauty that endures.

May we come to a time-honored, better destiny,
when we have moved beyond the bonfire and clear-cut mind
of wasting without thought
> in our ever-growing degradation
> of fine, skilled, honest labor.

May we see a new America that comes into the humble grace
> of things well built,
> well cared for, and

deserving of our children's children.

Grama

Your life will be reordered when you live the desert seasons,
for summer follows winter here, with spring delayed
    for dust and wind.
Going from cold to hot makes for
many disagreeable defenders of their cause (and people too).
    The spiny mace of cholla,
    the agave's needle ends,
    the burrs and bites and burns of spiders,
    plants, and ants.
But among the great defenders stands a humble,
    defenseless thing,
    though domineering in its will.
It bears the drought of dry, cold winters
    with grey tones as sad as any blue note.
But when the heat of May has passed, the late June shower
    moves the gray to nibs of green,
and cattle, deer, and antelope join happy dogs
    along their day-worn path
to nibble grass as fresh as water from a spring.
And when the rains of its summer growth have fed
its seeding heads, it moves to autumn's amber shades.
The amber is now gray again.
    The creatures await the cycle
for that perfect rainy season, when for all,
    the grass is green and freely given.

Epiphany and the Church of God—Amtrak

"I believe in Jesus, so I can walk on water. See, Daddy, I can walk on the sea."

These were the words of a young child, six years old, as she waited for the train in the Houston Amtrak station. The floor there was a scuffed and less-than-shiny sea blue linoleum tile (since replaced). How marvelous that a child should see it as the crystal blue sea and be carried in her imagination to the story of Jesus walking toward his disciples, as this small child walked on the tile sea to her daddy.

Just as I started writing this about her, so that I wouldn't forget what she'd said, here was this same child, standing in front of me, with the biggest, tight-lipped, toothless grin she could muster.

"What's your name?" I asked.

All I got back was bright eyes and that silly grin. Off she went, but in a moment, she was back again—same grin.

Again, I said, "What's your name? I guess you're not going to tell me, are you?" I'll never know.

As someone who travels frequently, usually in airports, I have found that riding the train offers a kind of epiphany. It is a contemplative experience—if you allow it.

Airport holding areas, otherwise known as gates, are packed with anonymity, constant announcements over ubiquitous speakers about not smoking, abandoned baggage, security threat levels, changed gates, boarding announcements, TVs on different channels, and the airports' own announcements about the pride they take in their airport and their city. One can sit next to someone for two hours and never exchange a smile or a word—or for that matter, find two minutes when the ambient noise is low enough to even attempt a conversation with someone not already on a cellphone or plugged into a headset.

But waiting for the train in downtown Houston, one experiences an entirely different slice of life. No muzak. The only announcements are for the actual arrival of the train, but that is usually anticlimactic, because inevitably, there is a young child waiting at the door. Keeping a watchful eye, a young boy was the first to see the train coming, and he yelled, "The train is coming! The train is coming!" I don't have to envy his enthusiasm because he offers it as a gift to all of us.

While people wait for an hour or two for the train to slowly roll in, strangers talk to strangers. They watch a mother's children as she, traveling alone with her children, steps outside for a smoke. Any distinction of class or race seems to melt away in the most relaxed way we might ever encounter in our divided world. It is truly an amazing experience.

The first time, it seemed it might be a fluke. But this ritual of grace-filled waiting has been repeated at 9 p.m. in downtown Houston, Texas, Friday after Friday. People get on with designer luggage, broken-down suitcases, plastic bags, and everything in between—many things the airlines would never permit.

Once on the train, confessions come in the dining car as you sit with complete strangers. One is a survivor of Katrina. Another is trying to start a new life without heroin. What do you say? All I could say to my sole companion at the dinner table at that moment, the recovering addict, was, "Our culture makes it very hard to forgive yourself." And before I might have thought to add, "I hope that you can," it seemed that those unspoken words had been spoken by the Spirit. She wept. And when I recalled later our brief moments in each other's lives, I wept.

Epiphany is celebrated as the recognition of God in human form. I give thanks for the Epiphany of grace made manifest by (as Paul would say) the Church of God—Amtrak.

Planned to Death
(A reflection on the documentaries, *The Unforeseen* and *Planet Earth*)

We all know. You're the only one that doesn't.
Like the Texas woman standing on the Capital grounds,
we proclaim the eminent domain of our rights
    over every other creature.
Humans at the top—damn whatever comes below us,
be it bear or bird or bug. The "land developer"
lays out the plan in no uncertain terms,
    "I'll be goddamned if anybody is gonna tell
    me how many houses I can build on this land."
We are the great sculptors of the landscape, with our
master-planned communities of cheap construction
and bankrupt vision, where the books
only record the credits of
    profit, pride, and
    greed and
never render the debits to water, farmland, creatures,
to lives robbed of their
    joy and beauty and peace.
Humility and context, lost in the grandeur of the plan.
Pouring ribbons of cement mile after mile to move
impatient passengers from boredom to boredom,
we pour into the countrysides of Texas, California,
Florida, Georgia—jobs on one end of the road,
    our bedrooms on the other.
Nothing in between but road rage, Walmart, and car dealers.
    "Master plans" that have ignored
    their Master to the peril of all.

The vastness and splendor of a created world
lies beyond our mind, mired as it is in
    our senseless stupidity and destruction.
Blind we remain to the persistent hope—the gratitude of life
lived out instinctively, beautifully, in grace perfected—

>   of the panda
>   of the polar bear
>   of the emperor penguin.
>
> Creatures each given to a hardship of existence for which we,
> in our malnourished philosophic quest,
> would render not worth the effort. Pass then,
>   creatures of the ice and snow
>   into the annals of extinction,
> where later regret can bring no resurrection.
> If what we do brings you to this fateful end, so be it.
> We've saved you the trouble of struggling on.
> Besides beauty, what do you have to offer us?
> Where is your value-proposition that we can
>   exploit for our profit, anyway?

Cultivate the heart of gratitude, Ms. Ellen Davis
tells us. To cultivate anything of lasting worth,
    we need the humus, the water, the sun, the dung,
the honest labor and honest accounting of lives well lived.
    Eyes wide open to the free gifts of creation.
Hearts beating in compassion for the
    common good of the
    common humanity for the
    common welfare
of fish and fowl, beast and reptile, forest and
    desert, ocean and mountain.
Ears peeled to birdsong, winds, and the vast
silences of God. Hands unclenched in generosity
and friendship of all. Tongues tired of the lies,
    tired of the excuses,
    tired of the empty optimism of empire—
Ready instead to sing the indwelling Spirit's
    litany of gratitude.
A song too long repressed.

And so, the grateful heart returns once again to the Garden

and strolls in the shade of the warm summer day
    with the Master Planner of the Master Plan,
and we see, what has always been there,
    what we have known all along,
even in our blindness.
    For indeed, "It is good."

The Wrong of Rights
(A reflection on the writings of Raimond Gaita and Simone Weil on the idea that the fight for "rights" is the fruit of compromise for the full dignity of our common humanity)

Stack them up whatever way you want.
Add to, subtract from—they never balance.
My rights may be a wrong to some.
    (I know they are!)
Your right's a wrong to me.
    (Pray God, forgive me my trespasses.)
Where does my right start and where does it end?
A piece of paper declares I own
a pinhead-sized piece of this solar system.
Do I, in my pinheaded mentality, do whatever I want
    with it,
    to it,
    on it—as is my right?
Does a corporation, as a person, have that same right?
    (Well, of course it does, you fool!)
    (Deliver us from evil.)
Land rights, women's rights, victims' rights, Black
rights, religious rights, gay rights,
    animal rights (underrepresented in the electorate)—
all clamoring for access to individualism's
    self-righteous control.

(Why didn't Jesus stake his claim for Messiah's rights?)

The only way to right the wrongs of
    the rights denied,
    the rights abused,
    the rights misused,
is to take rights off the scales once and for all.
    (Yes, and for all!)
Let us be rid of the scales of justice that have,

for too many millennia, been weighted with the heavy thumb
of power ever tilting toward justice veiled—justice denied.
Put them in the museums so that future generations may
know of their faulty reckoning for humanity's common fate.
    Simplify the legal code.
Make no law that steals one's dignity for another.
Make no law that leaves the world diminished
    for those that follow.
Make no law that gambles the welfare of creation
    for the profit of the few.
Make no law of compromise where common humanity
    lies precariously in the breech.
End the worship of exclusion, of class, of creed,
of greed, of pride, of cause, of party, of nation
    (as we forgive those who trespass against us).

    Bring the leaven of dignity
to knead into the bread of our humanity.
Plant seeds of uncompromising gentleness, restraint,
    sympathy, affection.
Celebrate color without racial caricature.
Celebrate culture without sectarian division.
Celebrate marriage as an intimate bonding to community
    without the bishop's and government's interference.
Celebrate economic opportunity in its simplicity without
    the exploitation that ignores the wheel of life.
Celebrate the end of the politician
as the answer to our problems,
as we celebrate at last the indivisible connection *of* all
acted upon with every deed and every word *by* all
ensuring liberty, justice, and dignity *for* all—
    imperishable from the earth.
    (Thy Kingdom come.)

Mission of Dignity

Impressing ourselves and society, we give gifts,
awards, honorary doctorates, medals of honor
to impress the actors, politicians, CEOs.

Protecting ourselves and society, we take a hard
line on immigrants to the south beyond our borders
to protect us from Mexicans, Haitians, Guatemalans.

Deceiving ourselves and society, we declare a
war on drugs and an unending war on terrorism
to deceive us into believing victory is somehow ours.

Oppressing ourselves and society, we set a minimum
wage that does not equate to a living standard
to oppress the work of scrubbing, picking, and cooking.

Destroying ourselves and society, we proclaim the
corporation a person without personal responsibility,
to destroy all accountability to the common good.

Confining ourselves and society, we incarcerate
the troubled, the mad, the drugged, the profiled,
to confine our justice to populist, formulaic tough talk.

Having impressed, protected, deceived, oppressed,
and destroyed, we have failed to ensure dignity
uncompromised for ourselves and society.

Turn, then, from want of more to want of
right and want of truth. Turn then, from
compromises costly ends to dignity ensured.

Ensure that we honor the labors of hard work,
simplicity, creativity, beauty—preserving in the most

sustaining way these free gifts of creation.

Ensure that we honor the alien, the neighbor at
home and abroad—honoring culture, subsistence,
agriculture—ways other than only our own.

Ensure that our society is based on health, as the
fundamental essence of life—celebratory wholeness
held in trust with all peoples of the world.

Ensure that we protect the most vulnerable and
protect ourselves from all-consuming greed—seeking
a living standard in harmony with the place and its people.

Ensure that corporations and global markets are
entities living within restraint—made accountable for
waste, exploitation, compromised safety, greed, and lies.

Ensure that even the most violent and deranged
are treated with inherent dignity—seeking always
the way to life affirmation, healing, and restoration.

Are these only the pious dreams of an overly pious, silly
mind? No, they are a call to action for the mission
work of dignity's claim on us for the survival of us all.

Thirty-one Haiku
Reflecting One Mind's Musing
Morning, Noon, and Night

Morning—Reflections on the Mind

I. Guilt

Energy spent small
Effort in pride's reduction
Enormous healing

II. Line in the Sand

Ethic bounds declared
Moral good un-compromised
Dignity ensured

III. Humility

Ego set aside
Pride as virtue lost at last
Grace perfected here

IV. Peace

More than absent war
Life taken in the balance
Creation's beauty

V. Fear

Controlling weapon
Commodity abundant
Not worth the effort

VI. Forgiveness Withheld

Denied as pure gift
The weight of burden ensured
Misery confirmed

VII. Love

Cynicism gone
Wasted energy regained
Smile given for all

IIX. Prayer

Into the ether
Whereabouts unknown for sure
Now into the heart

IX. Money Grubbers

Greed's ill-gotten gains
Enough is never enough
Enough is enough

X. Sin

Gives the preacher cause
The list varied by doctrine
Your list always long

Afternoon—Reflections on Nature

I. Dogs

Napping again now
Content to remain obtuse

Joy bestowed for free

II. Dust Storm

Beats relentlessly
Batters the weary senseless
Its own rest denied

III. Cactus Wren

Curiously wound
Inconvenient nesting ground
Joyful chirping sound

IV. Water

Clearly given to us
Muddied by misuse, abuse
Tainted by our greed

V. Snake

Rattle, no rattle
Harming fewer than we harm
Cursed into the dust

VI. Mountain Divide

Rising from the plain
Earth's proportion visible
Grandeur undenied

VII. Deer

Stealth wanderer here
Intrepid victim of cars

Carrion buffet

IIX. Quail

Funny little plume
Wobbling near the house for corn
Joined by all the rest

IX. Midday Sun

Bright light, bright blue sky
Makes paltry city skylines
Perfection given

X. Late Afternoon

Thunderstorm appears
Nature's power to create
Bravado—no rain

Evening—Reflections on Darkness

I. Streetlight

Not bad in concept
Ubiquitous in practice
Stars lost to its glare

II. Light at the End of the Tunnel

Roaring down the track
Hell if you get in its way
Or maybe heaven

III. Satellite

Our little twinkle
Streaking across the night sky
Not much grandeur there

IV. Venus

Sun's remaining gift
Holy nighttime's pronouncement
Time to watch the stars

V. Silence

Dog snoring aside
Nighttime silence filled with awe
Peace assured by dreams

VI. Cold Room

Sheets like ice again
No body could ever warm
Too warm to crawl out

VII. Splendor

Distant lighting flash
Eon's ions on display
Makes you feel alive

IIX. Nightmare

Daytime fears confirmed
Hope distills the logic lost
Passing fear released

IX. Open Window

Coyot' pups cry out
Echoes of the desert night
City sounds devoid

X. Dark Tranquility

Peace a promised claim
One poor species out of sync
Night and day the same

Mr. Corporation

You have usurped your purpose of outliving your inventors
and have overstepped your once-intended bounds.

Now, you are but bartered paper
with no purpose but for profit—bought and sold,
merged and plundered at the whim of CEOs.
With disregard for all things sacred,
you cry foul when asked to ponder future good.
    You grease the palms of politicians to ensure
    the tax rate suits your plan.
    You take to court
(to keep your interests) the very notion that you're a man—
yet you hide behind your paid-up lawyers
when the people want
    (for justice's sake) your manly flesh in jail.

Owning up is one sure measure you avoid
with purpose every day, but there are others
    just as troubling and corrupt.

The market holds declining labor as a good for products sold,
while boardrooms coldly justify your lavish ways.
In dollars, stocks, and options far beyond your paltry worth,
you rob the common good because you can.
You fly around the planet seeking markets for your wares,
always looking for some labor on the cheap.
    You tout your global presence
    while plundering the Earth's resources—
    fouling everything you see or seem to touch.
    You foul the air, you foul your nest,
    you foul your children's children's nest.
You've lost the vision of ensuring corporate good
    to a vision of corporate all.
You show the world a glossy image

with foundations built on lies.
You trade moral good for ill-got gains—
investing tainted gains in funds to gain still more.
You speculate on speculation as the spectacle continues
    with the parties your blind partners in disguise.
Trading grain and grabbing land, you steal
the bread from mothers' hands
as you settle some odd score for always more.

Depriving dignity to billions,
you celebrate your greatness and inclusion in the club
of those who have—condemning those you've chosen
    as have-nots.
You move from place to place,
never knowing your own home,
for homes are built with love and peace and grace.
    In the end, you are no human soul
    but only what we feared.
The shadow of temporal man's unfettered greed.

Left, Right, and Center

I'm not a party loyalist.
How anyone can be in our media-blitzed day
    is a mystery to me.
Listen to a debate of the party loyalists who jab and
stab while promising change and bi-partisan cooperation,
and one quickly sees
    how shallow the words and
    how deep the lies.
Promises made and promises broken, yet always the
promise of regaining American greatness,
as though one person could offer such greatness
    to a nation.
As though we knew for certain
    what greatness they would impart.
It is but mere distraction
from the responsibilities of the people,
this search for their left, right, and center
    no party can endorse—
    lost as parties are in dividing "us" and "them."
They keep the volume high to drown out
the voices of the weak, the prophetic—
lest we find another way to humility and grace.

If we are to be the hope of a better-governed world,
let us find our leftist wing in caring for the poor and
engaging in labor's honest, sacred work.
Let us find our rightist wing
of a better conservatism that honors
    local investments in
    local businesses with
    local accountability and
    local conservation.
Let us find our center of egalitarian affection,

cultural celebration, uncompromised compassion,
    and sacred expression.
Let us see that we cannot live well walking a party line
    defined by money, power, and greed.
Let us see what we forfeit when we concede
our future to present-day lies.
Let us see a way forward,
moving from executive monarchs and
    beltway control to a million solutions
    in a million places
    for the millions gathered
in their unique and lovely places.
And where the lies have changed the lovely to the ugly,
let us rebuild our lives and places with the
    great care,
    great love, and
    great beauty
of the world given to us at creation's dawn.

God in a Box

Some who espouse an eternal god seem locked in
on locking that same god to a created world
produced in magic wonder in six days 6,000 years ago.
    I must admit, I do not see the point.
I, too, believe in an eternal god, though the god who rattles
around in my small mind has a much bigger vision
of creation, with its
    seeming infinity of stars
    in billions of galaxies,
    billions upon billions of rocks and
matter and creatures floating in an
incomprehensible realm of time.
I'm quite happy to ponder the many ways
We've found our way
    to the odd creatures that we've become.
That it remains well beyond my grasp to say
where we will be
    in a million or
    a billion years is fine with me.
I've neither the vision nor the patience to ponder much
    past my few score years.
Your god may be dead, if such ever was alive.
Mine alive, doing as it pleases.
Perhaps I'm really saddest for the god in one's small box.
For those with eyes wide open and awake,
behold a creation that
needs no defense by man
    of a god made small
    by fear and flimsy, faulty creed.

Flip the Switch

    What turns it on?
Weeks pass—nothing of substance appears.
Then, all of a sudden, come the words, pouring out
from some previously clogged up
    brain mass of pondering thought.
If the words are of use to some other is not of my concern.
If the creator has some use of them for others, so be it.
    If not, so be it.
    I write what has distilled
from some half century of observation,
    of trying to honor the prophet,
    of looking at the created world.
The words may not transform anyone else,
But it is as though the prayer has reached
    the great Creator
and come back to me refined. That grace perfected,
    freely given, is doing its work in my own soul.

(Thy will be done.)

Mascot
(For the curve-billed thrasher)

Where you nested before we built this place, I do not know.
Where you spent your days in observation before our time,
    again, I cannot say.
I rejoice that your little flock has made a home here with us,
nesting behind the light fixture underneath
    the overhang of our screened porch
        that somehow in your travels you discovered and
        chose for home.
From there you wander, flying from parapet to parapet
to get a different view and pronounce boldly
    your melodious invocation on the day.
You stay with us through the winters and the summers,
    and even through the fire—
Your tender hatchlings not always seeing many days.
You are our loyal mascot. A reminder of why we're here.
Celebrating desert days, nature's song, unexpected blooms,
dark skies, the Milky Way, distant peaks, and
    the lives of simple creatures, like yourself.

The Path

It's a long walk. I'm not sure I have the strength.
    Not walked, I know I'll never move.
So up I go and out the door—if only I had the enthusiasm
of the dogs. All they need is the click of the leash and,
no matter the weather or the mood, they race to the door
to sniff the trail and look for anything worth
    pulling off toward.
    Perhaps I'll trust their instinct that with the walk
comes strength and vigor
as surely as two canines clearly show.
    Press on, dear pilgrim,
    for the path that lies ahead,
    though rough and hard,
will bring you to the grace of life well lived.

State of Confusion
(Reflections on the 2012 State of Union speech by President Obama with quotations from the speech)

Are we that easily fooled? I guess perhaps we are.
    "Anyone who tells you that America is in
    decline or that our influence has waned,
    doesn't know what they're talking about."
The cheering of our greatness presses on without
restraint as we offer, "decisive blows against our
enemies." From Pakistan to Yemen, the operatives
    remain a-scrambling, knowing they can't
    escape the reach of USA.
The bravado song continues of a warring peoples'
mood, as we talk of heroes worshipped in utter
blind allegiance to a lie. World leaders pay their
homage, as though they had a choice. They, too,
need the lie to keep it going. But in truth, we're
hated greatly by many in the world or envied for
    our treasure chests of gold and guns and grit.

Open more resources for our oil and gas resources!
The cry goes out to plunder nature more. We're
never called to alter our wasteful, wonted ways, for
first must come the assurance of always more.
    The sun,
    the corn,
    the frac'ing gore,
    the wind,
    the waves on teaming shore
can never quench the thirst
    for lives of greed.
And yet we barter for the privilege
of squandering our tomorrows
as we drill and pump and burn and bulldoze sacred lands.
Across the aisle, it is no better,

as each invokes the Creator's blessing
while mocking that creation with their horrors.

The election cycle spinning, the promises come easy,
as the parties with their pundits assure us all again—
    the long deception that we are great.
In the end, it's just more spending
for bling that leads us nowhere whole
    except to our
    rightful, prideful,
    sinful, sad demise.

American Credo
i.
Put a sticker on the car—that should do the trick.
    Support the Troops!
    Our slogan for the flag—
    jingoism's credit for the debit of your life.
Our presidents would take a shotgun to a fly, or
so it seems. A fool's idea of a justified response—
killing men and towns and reason across the sacred earth.
    Their evil they unleash
on boys and girls and mothers, too—
anyone who happens in our way.
    In the wake
    of rubble and despair,
    sacrifice forgotten,
we offer nothing for the fray—
you alone must bear the burden and the cost.
For us, it's only dollars that feed the bottom line
while piling up the debt for those to come.
You reenter our world wounded, whether visible or not,
carrying hatred and fear and shadows
    in the night and in the day.
    Lurking, stalking, terrifying
not only you but also those you love,
as the switch to turn it off seems broken, too.
And if we drive you mad enough,
    we'll label you dishonorable,
sparing us the obligation of your care.
    Our talk is cheap, our violence real,
    our care for you a mere token of our shame.
In the end, you alone bear our greed and condescension
    as you wander,
    soulless, lost,
    in war's cruel end.

ii.
There is only one economy. The economy of evermore.
The politician promises jobs as we grow the economy
in growing measure with
    our growing greed and
    growing debt,
    our growing corruption and
    our growing waistlines.
Our cities grow on farmland lost. New megastores replace
the diminished wealth of small shops
and livelihoods, leaving in their wake
a derelict reminder of a more graceful way, now lost.
A city's economic growth is many a small town's demise.
    (The net of our deeds remains off the corporate books.)
Such is the capitalistic way of blind regard.
    Our disturbing presence in the world
seeks to export our blinded ways to the greedy in every land.
We have lost humility to the pride of might makes right.
But our might makes little right
and much more deadly wrong.
    Indeed, the meek shall inherit the earth,
    for they are its rightful heirs.
    For where they see goodness,
corrupted man seeks only goods for sale.

iii.
Despite Irving Berlin's chorus rousing our tear-filled eyes,
I see no reason why God should bless America.
We have squandered every gift this good land has given us:
    majestic mountains;
    lakes of pristine waters;
    primordial forests with all their creatures;
    grasslands, farmlands, and people, too.
From the mountains to the valleys to the oceans
    white with plastic,

we have grabbed and burned and overturned the order of a
grace-filled land—filtering out the light above with our
polluted metroplex conglomerations
of concrete, steel, and glass.
    I can never, in my prayer, utter, "God damn America,"
as I cannot ask Perfected Love to undo its just perfection.
But if I am to pray to Love for the justice that is due,
    I pray we find our way from desecration to
the sacred trust of all that is—
in this fine land and all fine lands
    of God's rich, glorious earth.

Angels of Our Nature
(A reflection on the nurses, chaplains, social workers, and others who work to restore to health the soldiers around the world).

Entering as you do with the bandages of mercy,
you are involved in the most important and labored task
of caring for the wounded souls of soldiers.
These men and women,
    coming out of the shadows of imprisoned hearts,
extend their hands for healing.
    Too often, there is no hand there for them.
We burden you with the immense task of binding them up
for some better, more peaceful day.
Your healing, compassionate touch
offers them tenderness and consolation
in the dark and difficult times
    with their questions,
    doubts,
    fears, and
    suffering.
As you use your hands, your heart and faith
to care for these in need of God's protection,
pray that God will continue to grace you
with a servant's heart
that will nurture, strengthen, and challenge you
    to see as God sees
    —in the heart.

Aperture to the World

The panorama of Creation is too vast for us to grasp.
Our aperture to the world restricts a greater view.
Yet that constriction is largely our own choosing,
as we seek an ever-narrowing field of vision that we can
    control in our smallness,
    our fears,
    our illusions and delusions.
May we open up the aperture to the blinding
light of abundance, to feed us and sustain us for the task.
Wake up, old souls, and see before us the grace-filled task of
    loving,
    caring,
    nurturing,
beyond our wildest vision!

Just as the tiny monarch and the great blue whale
each travel a thousand miles with no assurance of return,
may we, too, wander forth within our lives,
ever freed from the limitations of prejudice and hate.
    And so we find a grace perfected
in the storm and in the stillness,
in the creatures in their pastures,
in the oceans and the deserts
    of this created earth. A grace for life.
A grace for peace. A grace for all.

The Ant and Her Man

You seem to think the paths I clear are tracts
designed for you as you move your mound
out of the grass and right into the middle of my good work.
    Well, that suits me well enough.
I can walk around you while marveling at your homestead.

You know your place and you keep it well.
Not like your tiny little cousins, who like
to set up the daily migration into kitchen
and closet through invisible passageways.

No, you do your good work out in the open—
looking for whatever might be useful. And
any of those pesky grasshoppers you
can haul back to the mound for your winter
stores, you have my blessing to sting with your
deadly sting and have for yours alone.

    (I wish we had more of you and fewer of them).

It gives me some joy to think that the cleared path
    has given you
the unobstructed morning view of the beautiful
desert plateau you call home with your several thousand kin.
    You outnumber us, outwork us,
and will no doubt out-survive us.
    Harvest on, quiet laborer.
    Harvest on.

End-times Schizophrenia

If the Creator wants to de-create all that was created
on Earth in a final, fiery flash of the great apocalypse,
    my paltry opinions on the matter won't matter much.
But it seems to me that, after millennia of waiting for the
    end of it all, we might just as well get of one mind
and make a go at treating creation with due respect—
talked about often enough—rarely practiced.
    It has birthed us,
    sustained us,
    inspired and confounded us.
But it has never produced another creature so disjointed
    in its mind from its place.
The followers of one young Galilean mock his admonition
to do the work to make Earth heaven.
    (Lest we call the man a fool for suggesting
    that the kingdom come on Earth as in heaven).
The Creator thought the job was done,
    declaring all things good,
before we wrote a different tale of woe
    to justify our ends.
"This generation shall not pass away"
is not a call to have disdain for this life
    for some future form.
It is a call to sort out our many conflicting minds
    to be of one mind with
    creation and its creatures—
    brothers and sisters of assorted creeds and cultures—
with our own mind, as it finds, finally, its own
    peace on Earth, goodwill to all.

On a Line from Daniel Koh

Where can I find you?
    "Mired in the dusty corners of the library"
—lost among shelves of knowledge, information, data.
Some priceless, some seemingly a waste of trees.
Gathering words and numbers and
images on our quest for wisdom
    to impress, to inspire,
    to coerce, to persuade
(sometimes others, sometimes ourselves),
we lose ourselves in wonder and imagination among
the bound-up versions of another's mind. The pages offer us
    truths to ponder,
    veiled lies of deceit,
    windows to the soul,
    steel doors to reason,
    madness manifest in ink,
    grace transcending breath.
We write, we read, we seek. But why?
    Mired in the dusty corners of the mind,
the pilgrim ponders the choice—seeking an illusory self
    or seeking love.
    Where can I find you?

Daydream
(A reflection on a question of Thomas Merton on the lives of the "religious")

"How deep does the decency go?"
On the right, the cry goes out for
    the right to life;
    family values;
    allegiance to might;
    power to the free market.
On the left, the universal daydream continues for
    life defined by court-approved rights;
    regulation defined by law;
    attachment to many causes.
But the decency of left and right is only skin deep.
Cut into the flesh of each and out spills the blood
    of corruption,
    of ineptitude,
    of cynicism,
with ever-present signs of dis-ease.

The seven deadly sins, alive and well—tainting all they touch.
Our right to life applying only to the innocent,
    as defined by us.
    Our family values
a mockery of the common good of a people.
    Our jingoism under stars and stripes
assailing distant cultures
    and our own poor and lost and lonely.
Our trade and commerce stealing,
plundering, and masking endless greed.

Apathetic citizens too are alive,
though the bones are being shaken.
For the paltry rights attained from the battles of our times
    still deny a common humanity indivisible to all.

Our free choices have left us
with little good to choose from,
as the age continues its stronghold on our fantasies.
The complicity of the consumerist lifestyle,
begging for loopholes tailored to confirm
    the status quo's momentum.
Fighting for some cause gives cheap relief of guilt assuaged,
while never opening wholeheartedly to the brighter dawn.

Reexamine decency, then, and see that it is lost.
The right to life is not a possession
    to be given by some, taken from others.
The values of family are instilled only in a community of love.
The true allegiance is to our interconnected lives in creation.
The only free market is the recognized dignity of good work
and the laborer worthy of hire.
The court cannot ensure that you have done your part
    in upholding the uncompromised dignity of all.
Our selfishness can never attain goodness when
    individualism trumps the common good in
    condescension's wake.
Our lifestyle cannot demand laws for regulation
that our shopping sprees and automobiles continue to defy.
We cannot reconcile some narrow cause with its own
    destructive effect and end.

If we are to come to peace in this world,
we must move past the universal daydreams and illusions,
with their pathetic pundits extolling tactics of diversion.
We must move past the arrogance of answers,
    the pride of assurances,
    the pandering to our fears,
    the giddy optimism cheaply peddled,
to the humility of questions and doubts instilled with hope.
    For in the end,
we are all seekers. The way to destruction is broad,

the gate to life narrow. Take action for a better day.
Visit the old men and women shut up
    and lonely in their years.
Open your table to those who you would judge
    and hear their story.
Instead of buying landfill junk, build something
    crafted with care.
Instead of marching in angry protest,
    sit in quiet contemplation,
pondering your own complicity in the violence of our world.
Wake up from the daydream of
    universal despair,
    universal exploitation,
    universal overexposure to the noise.
Quiet your heart and your mind for a simpler life,
    more grace-filled,
    more in context with your place,
    more open to the other.
In so doing, we will need less and want less
of the right and left's ill direction, powered
by our blind devotion and complacency.
We will awaken to the beauty of the
    restored fence row and tiny stream,
    small orchard and city garden patch,
colors, sounds, and affections of the gatherings around us,
    innocence of children deserving of a better future.
And in these simple acts of faith, we will finally bear
    decency in our very core.

The Amish and the Church of God–Amtrak

While I was attending Anderson College, I became active in the Church of God—Anderson, Indiana. There, I learned that there was an altogether different Church of God—the Church of God—Cleveland, Tennessee. It's only been in the past couple years that I learned of a third Church of God, and I consider myself a member of a kind: the Church of God—Amtrak. In an earlier meditation, I mentioned my experiences of epiphany as I waited for the Friday night train in downtown Houston. The diversity and grace to be found there is quite remarkable at times.

On a Friday night in May 2010, two older Amish couples and two boys, pretty obviously brothers, about ten and twelve years of age (probably grandsons of one of the couples) came into the Houston station to buy their tickets. They had not gone "online" to make a reservation—they had just shown up. The ticket agent, rather than just dispense with his duties, wanted to know all about them. The rather extroverted leader of the group was glad to go into how the Amish could generally recognize where another Amish was from by dress, beards, and surnames.

These particular Amish were from the center of the state in Missouri. "We were here to lead about two dozen young schoolteachers do some work in Galveston," he explained. "This is our fourth trip since last fall."

Too bad these people don't get cable news. They would have known that the media had long lost interest in the rebuilding of Galveston from Hurricane Ike in 2008. It says something about a community when it keeps returning to help when there is nothing in it for them, as we measure the world. In fact, they spend their hard-earned money to get here and leave their livelihoods behind to work for free long after most "relief efforts" have moved on. And they don't go to make converts. Their missionary work is about service, and they serve a culture that shows nothing but contempt for all their ways. Despite this, these "odd" ways have preserved their small communities.

There was no rush for tickets, and the ticket agent was in no rush to pass these eccentrics their tickets and be done with them. Behind the glass window, I could hear little of what he said, but it led to the Amish man adding, "Yes, in fact, on one trip to New Orleans, a man there who I had worked with for many weeks after Katrina loved my straw hat. 'I sure wish I had me a hat like that,' he told me. So I took off my hat and signed my name on the inside of it and said, 'Here, this is yours.' He just started crying. When I talked to him not too long ago, he said he had that hat hanging on his wall."

He explained that they were taking the long way home. "Gonna ride the train all the way to Los Angeles and then take another train back toward home. We love riding the train. We'll be home in a week."

Amongst themselves, they spoke low-Dutch with an interesting mix of English thrown in. These worldly Missouri Amish didn't look like the Holmes County, Ohio, Amish. Neither man had a beard. Everyone had a head covering, as one would expect, but for the two young boys, these were black fedoras. They looked more like Al Capone sidekicks than Amish boys, except for their simple farm clothes and suspenders. Practicality was not lost on them either. The two older women both wore black sneakers.

After a week in a hotel room, watching a 24-hour news cycle on who should be blamed for the oil mess in the Gulf, I was taken back to the words of Martin Luther King, Jr. from *Beyond Vietnam*: "Rationalizations and the incessant search for scapegoats are the psychological cataracts that blind us to our sins. But the day has passed for superficial patriotism. He who lives with untruth lives in spiritual slavery. Freedom is still the bonus we receive for knowing the truth."

BP is not to blame, nor is Obama. The average person in the world uses 2,000 watts of energy per year. In Switzerland, it is 5,000 watts. In America, it is 12,000 watts.

Two things came to me this evening as I boarded my Amtrak ride home. One was, if anyone is not to blame, it is the Amish, who have lived with a conservation of resources we can't fathom. The second was, when the news cycle is over and everyone else has moved on from this tragedy, the Amish may well be back in south Louisiana or Texas, once again putting lives back together for cultures they reject.

The Boys and Ego—Return on Investment (ROI)

Overwhelmed with little purpose—perhaps none—
we have made ourselves busy in the running of our lives.
Busyness suggests purpose and demands its pursuits:
    Pursuit of wills;
    Pursuit of happiness;
    Pursuit of more;
Pursuit of importance as measured by the crowd.
    (Boring, really.)
Hope replaced by optimism. Peace by ulcers and
workouts at the gym, as we pursue in vain
    cinema's perfected image.
Our community service is calculated
for its ROI, to make a better resume.
Introductions and handshakes deliberate acts of
    attaching self-importance to the deed.
Talking always of investments, sports, sex.
Making fantasy connections with the blond across the bar
and passing innuendo with the gang.

When the boredom has run its course, the pursuits exhausted,
the odd-man-out appears the wiser soul. Like Jayber Crow,
unconcerned about "making something of his life," he finds it
better to mutely listen
    when the others brag and boast.
    Preferring poetry over journals,
and starlit nights over nightclubs—
he comes easier to a pace of
deliberate rest and consolation, offering to him
    greater care,
    greater understanding,
    greater patience.
A resonance is heard (for those who listen) with
    the Creator and its being, who is,
finally, whole, at rest, and at peace in this good world.

Forgive My Lack of Originality

My redundant self gathers words,
defining in the days and in the nights the events of
    a country
    a religion
    a landscape and place
written down so as to connect the dots
    of the pondering tangles of thought.
Reread to keep the mind attached to soul.
    Shared in the hope of connecting soul with soul.

Ideal's Reality

The ideal was once expressed as better for
nine guilty to go free than for one innocent
person to be convicted wrongly. Such ideals
never have been our true and fullest history,
but at least we told ourselves
    that we believed in such.

Now, we have abandoned even the notion
of such an ideal. The new ideal is no ideal.
We've finally made the reality our ideal.
Better to kill a dozen children
    than let one Taliban live.

Such is our progress in democracy.

Answerman

Dear God, I heard the radio preacher say that not all
the Bible was to be read literally —
    just 99.9%.

(I'd have to do the math, but I'd guess that 0.1% refers to
to selling all you have and giving it to the poor. He didn't
specify).

He sold you, God, as the god of hoops that his
forty-five years of studying the Bible gave him,
"knowledge" to assure the crowd.
He even had chapter and verse to prove it.
    (Imagine that!)
    It was clear:
If we didn't jump through the proper hoops, soon
    the rapture would leave us behind.
With such complex and contradictory instructions,
hell is indeed a crowded place, as we have made
    Your good creation into hell itself.
Jesus didn't seem to do much hoop-jumping,
preferring always to juggle
the religious establishment's hoops
    more for entertainment
    than for attainment.

(The Sabbath was made for man not man for the Sabbath.)

Forgive us our silliness as we forgive the silliness of others.

Elegy to Johnny Graf (1924–1993)

    Enigma.
Perhaps I was such a thing to you
as you were in some part to me.
You always wanted a "preacher" in the family,
even though you slept through more
    Sunday sermons than not.
You even offered to pay for seminary if I'd go.

(You never knew, but I almost took you up on that.)

Yet you never told us of your great-grandfather,
    August Graf,
who served his little congregation without pay for
    thirty-five years: 1883–1918.
Or how his parents died when he was seven and
left Switzerland when twenty-one for Fulton County.
    Maybe you didn't know.

On our countless trips to the Rupp's in Pettisville,
we drove by the Ayers and Smith cemeteries,
both only a few miles from our farm
and right across the road from each other,
where most of your father's and mother's
relatives were buried, including August,
    yet we never stopped
and the connection was never mentioned.
    I'd like to ask you about them now.
It's often too late by the time we think of
all the questions we'd like to ask about
    those gone before.
Maybe none of us expressed any interest
    in the dead, though it must be said,
your wife traipsed me around Pettisville Cemetery
visiting parents, grandparents, aunts, uncles,

her baby sister, neighbors, and friends.

    In the intervening years,
I've learned a lot about the Graf and Schudel,
Winzeler and Merillat lines that brought you forth.
I've done what I can to pass along
    to your children and grandchildren
    the good and bad and in-between.

You taught me a notion filled with simple wisdom:
"At least if they are talking about me, I know
they are not talking about someone else."
You understood, if struggled to always live,
    the wise fact
that if we don't transform our pain,
    we are bound to transmit it.

I never went to seminary like you'd hoped,
    though your only daughter did.
Still, I preached at the little church in Marfa
for a few years. And I've written much
about God and Church and family and country.
    All these might still render me an enigma
to your experiences and sensibilities.
    I hope not.

In some way, I feel connected to those dead
in Smith and Ayers and elsewhere, as I do to
those Rupp and Beck, Vonier and Gearig
lines you betrothed yourself to for life.

You couldn't master patience for others,
    and even less for yourself—
your wife suggesting you stop praying for
patience, as it seemed God enjoyed the
opportunity to test it all the more.

But you taught and lived fidelity.
You showed us that love doesn't require perfection.
It just requires doing the chores
    day in and day out,
        whether in the mood or not.

Odd Fits

Food producers can't get in sync,
serving up as they do square buns with round burgers
    and square burgers with round buns
or round burgers lost in a larger round bun.
So it is with our lives. The meat inside never quite fits
    with the bread we put over it.
But how appetizing our life is to others depends
on the flavor of our grace and
not the perfection of the package.

    (You want fries with that?)

Fragments of Our Myth

Two American images of cinematic mythic proportion—
    Tara and Oz-bespeak ever-distant
dreams of our happiness and self-delusion. Tara imagined
    in some (white) perfected grandeur that never was,
    the Ozian Wizard in techno-pseudo-power.
Neither real. Both persisting in our minds.

u-a-p

Ponder facts instead of truths,
seeking knowledge over wisdom,
    and you shall find yourself
in sloth's ubiquitous-analysis-paralysis.

Lotto Fever

The greater the odds, the more we seem to think
the gambling gods will favor our pursuits.
When the mega-millions hits half a billion,
the people buy, in frantic madness, their big chance
    to be transformed by greed's cahoots.
It's hard to know who loses most—
    the winners or the losers.

Crimson Seas

For all the talk about peace,
for all the prayers for peace,
we are not a people of peace.
    I'm not, and you are not.
The politician and the preacher are not, either.
If we want peace, we have to stop fighting, and
as long as ego pursuits preside over our minds,
there are always more fights to fight, in our ambition
to become the great heroes of peace.
    Fights for our sovereignty.
    Fights for our security.
    Fights for rights and justice.
    Fights to fight the good fight with all our might.
    Fights for nation, god, and creed.
It seems our minds, made small
by history's crafted rendering,
cannot conceive of any path to peace but through
    the fight made right.

The preacher pounds the pulpit,
decrying the evil of our sins.
    "Fight, we must, the devil
and the temptations of the flesh.
Fight, we must, them who are not us!"

Some old man who has heard it once too often
asks the preacher for a word, "You've been
fighting all your life. When are you going to love?"

Formulating dignity with starched-like hair and coat and tie,
the politician mounts the stage to read
    the tele-prompter's formulated calculated lies.
    "I'm here to fight for you!

Fight against drugs, loose sex, and porno, too.
Fight against environmental wackos
    and terrorists and illegals who
have stolen your jobs and threaten your big dreams."

Always one election away from victory and its
    empty promise of peace sustained.
The soldier in the wheelchair hears again the dressed-up lies
    but is honored for his duty all the same.
He weeps tears of bitter anguish as the crowd
cheers ever on in orchestrated-manipulated-capitulated glee.

If we really want peace, what must we give up?
Is the price too costly for our world?
    No fight or battle or war.
    No lash or stone or noose.
    No finger or fist or scowl.
A hard list, and we've only just begun.
    No hatred or condescension.
    No greed or exploitation.
Apply those as you may to people, place, or thing,
skipping even one keeps the cycle spinning in its
never-ending gloom and doom;
blood and guts; greed and gain.
    Back to the fight we go!

There is another way,
one we have known 2000 years or more.
    A way that honors love and trust and grace.
It calls us to protect creation without any hesitation,
And calls on each to honor labor's hours.
It begs the Church doors open wide
to welcome, heal, and comfort any
    who may wander in its midst.
For families, love must rule where pride now hangs its hat—
vulnerable and open with imagination and affection—

    allowing each to be what God can see as good.

Such a way may always be the narrow gate, as we have seen,
    confined as it is by the gentle, peaceful, humble way.
It will not push or force or steal
to gain its edge on all our madness.
It is only realized by thought and word and deed wholly
    given over to thrift and to constraint,
    given over to the common good.
For it is in common humanity's claim within our
    common creation
that integrity, wisdom, and mystery at last prevail.
The ground, on which in peace we plant our feet,
brings us back to Earth itself—heart-whole and healed.
Akin we are to a Sequoia
    rooted firmly in the humus that feeds it,
    reaching to the light that brings it growth,
    the air made new as it passes through,
and whose final death by fire or decay returns its life to earth.
This should not surprise us, as our carbon is the same, and
the countless atoms bind our life and death as one.

Or perhaps we can admit that such is not our wish and
declare for all the world what dwells within.
We like the profit, the bravado, the battle, and the war,
the blood and gore, with all its powers to destroy.
    To hell with peace! Fight on! It's the only way we know.
Our pride resides in standing tough and tall.

And so Christ's wounds shall go on bleeding until
our species blood is drained into the dead crimson seas,
where hate and fear and justified defense
    have drowned all creation's sacred trust.
 Forgive us, Lord. We know not what we do. Though
    what we do, we know is surely wrong.

Oh, Sophia

Wisdom was given your sweet feminine name.
Perhaps that is why men have paid you little mind.
United they stand against you to prevail in sheer stupidity,
    year after year and
    millennium upon millennium.
Oh, Sophia, we need you more than we want you,
    mired as we are in ideologies of consent.
May we drink from the bosom of your sweet perfection,
    Oh, Sophia, oh, Sophia.

Heavenly Drone

What a knack you have for sweetness,
and how you find the latest blooms, I just don't know.
I've never seen your hive and never seen you swarm,
but you are there after rain's release of
    the cenizo's pink profusion on display.
You bring on dimensions of sound in flight
as you move from bloom to bloom with all your kind—
    so grand, so small, so gloriously divine.

Forgive us for usurping your good name
with our foul sinful deeds.
    Our buzzing drones leave wakes of death and fear.
While your gentle buzz offers all rich honey in the comb.

Credo in Unum Deum

I. Protestant Idolatry

You smashed the stained-glass windows.
Paintings that offended, you did burn.
You even crushed fine statues into finest dust—
    Blessed Mary
a stumbling block to your narrow brand of truth.
Constricts of your mind, so obsessed with idol worship,
you have traded glass and paint and stone for
    outlined pages locked in time.
    Now, the Bible stands as idol in your worship,
denying grace its perfect place within your mind.
And the offering plate is passed
    for programmatic business over art—
    mystery denied by the verbose.
Unity, so prayed for, remains caged within your walls,
    and even there, division finds a solid home.
Yet you, too, shall pass as you bid Sophia's call,
for dust thou art. And like the Virgin's image
that you ground to finest dust,
    to dust *thou* shalt return.

II. Catholic Folly

Your celibacy is commanded, opposing God's good ways—
    chastity a duty, not a gift.
You silence women and seclude them
in the roles that you define
while you measure out Christ's body to those
    aligned with all your rules.
Your boy's club keeps its grip on doctrine, creed, and deed
    with its schizophrenic family planning,
celebrating virtue while denying life's true passions.
    The truth you hold, you desecrate

behind corruption and abuse.
> *Anathema sit*

applies, it seems, to everyone but you.

III. Ordination's Limits

A degree may well define who is ordained and who is not.
> It may also be defined in canon law.

The checklist covers gender, age, and mental state—
though the measure of one's mind
> is tricky business, as we know.

We dare dole out the sacraments and blessings as it pleases
re-consecrating consecrated gifts of bread and wine—
made holy, once for all, 2,000 years ago or perhaps more,
> justly reckoned sacred at creation's dawn.

Sacrificial tithes and diversifying pensions keep
the game alive, while too often ignoring the Gospel work
> of caring for the poor.
> Wash the feet of passing strangers, if you hope to

live the rule—offering peace and grace and love
> for all you meet.

For your ordination is the call to serve and not to be served—
> to die to self

that others may see the grace-filled Way.

Oh, there was a simpler time when the Spirit made the call
and simply asked us, through the mystery and the smoke,
"Who will go for us?" And the answer that we offered
> came so meekly and sincerely,

"Here am I. Send me."

IV. Laity's Laziness

We like to park it in the pew, and let the others do the work.
Sunday's obligation wipes away

the propagation of our guilt—
    slothful shame from the books of the divine.
    We can't help it if we're lazy.
You've never trusted us for more, so less is
    what we've given now for years.
If you want our help, then ask us,
but don't expect too much.
    It takes a while to trust
the Spirit's whims, so long suppressed.
    Blow in Mighty Spirit, and
shake us from the pew, lest our dusty souls
    lie complacent to the end.

V. Church Authority

Does it bespeak the innocence in the Garden?
Does it bespeak God's mercy or our judgement?
Is the Bible a shield and the cross a sword or
    God's dynamic Word incarnate speaking to us still—
within, beyond history's leather-covered pages?
We have a chance to find the hope and dignity
that both creation and the cross ordained, but which has been
    compromised for not-so-pious power and control.
The measure of our lives is the grace we offer
    to the fringes and forgotten in our world,
not in our ongoing damning of the other.
The Church's authority is only real when it
    yields to forgiveness
    yields to humility
    yields to love.
All other forms may well be, if we will see,
    the Tempter's masterwork refined.

VI. Credo

I believe in fractals' mystery, a Creator so divine
that my small mind need only look beyond.
I believe in God made flesh as a way to life and truth,
though the truth is often hard to hear among the noise.
I believe in the Spirit's wiles, with its prophets and its seers
knocking reason on its backside just for sport.
I believe in love for all it offers,
with its gifts of grace and peace.
    I believe, you see, that God is God—
    whatever that may be.
I would even go so far as to confirm as simple fact
    that of God this can be said:
    I am not, and neither are you.

Summation

A familiar line, too long ignored—
What we do not cherish, we destroy.

The Ends

To some the prophet is clairvoyant—
    predicting what will come—
the words aligned to fit the latest plan.
What comes next we cannot know,
though for trying we might never
    yield the cause.
It suits our ego madness to sell a book or two
to buy that gated house we so deserve.

The prophet's wisdom runs another course from ours,
    or so it seems.
Knowing what will come is not knowing what
will come, when the means can change the ends
    for good or ill.
The prophet's words spell out for us the choices
we must make, while laying out the odds for us as well.
It's up to us to fulfill the evil that is there or
walk the other way, to God's good Grace.
    Stop predicting wrathful ends—
start living Love's one plan—that all should
    know the love of self for all.

Night Benediction

Now I lay me down to sleep.
The night is calm, the sky so deep.
Oh, gentle Spirit, bless this peace.
And in my death grant sweet release.

Glittering Diamonds

You are far more useful as tools
than on rings and things of serious bling.
The blood that bought your fame
has no claim on all that's good.
We can't deny your facet's splendor,
but for love's assurance, it's displaced.
You must be big; you must be gaudy
to prove your worth among the haughty.
Like other things in God's good world,
We've made your beauty
    the rich man's booty.

Told-ya-so

I didn't know it was a game of Told-ya-so,
but it seems to be the case. No matter
the point or lack thereof,
    the purpose is to play it.
I must be right—you must be wrong.
It's the same old, tired, boring song.

But if I'm not right and you're not wrong,
    perhaps we'll finally get along.

Just Desserts

A life in Church should teach us
    about the way to go.
Yet, something comes up missing
in the rule of life they show.
    We might learn all the stories.
    We might learn all the rules.
We might learn speculated consequences
    of a broken golden rule.
It's what we fail to learn that stirs me
about our pride and shame and blame.
And how our stubborn ways we carry
    cause loved ones to inflame.
We do not yield to Love's pure truth:
    That the merciful and meek
are the way to peace and truth,
    as the Perfected Son did speak.
Instead, we press and curse and deign to cede an inch
    of ego's glory,
        whose beauty is but ugliness
        dressed up in vanity's story.

We, the People

We, the people, elect the politicians we deserve.
For thus, beneath the fuss and muss,
    they look a lot like us.

Clingers

I am not a clinger. You know
the type I mean—hanging on friends
and lovers like cottonwood hangs on screen.

That nature shows such symbiosis is fine
to a degree, but as the kudzu kills the tree,
so too all this clinging kills dear me.

Hugging all they meet when a
handshake would do just fine.
Their self-worth all wrapped up
in clinging like a vine.

But even the most charged-up of us
will sooner or later be drained—
so approach us with all due caution
before you find yourself restrained.

Shake my hand and even hug me
if such closeness rules the day.
But please don't cling too close to me,
    or "Get off of me!" will I say!

Hell as Concept

Eternal torment, so much touted, is not a future place,
    but a state that was and is.
That it may well be, for fools like me,
    our sure and final destiny
surrenders hope before its time.

It is for those with eyes to see the evil of our day
to choose between the hopeless angst
    and God's more glorious way.

I shan't concede such cynicism as to have thus conferred
    hell upon the worst and vilest of our kind, as I might say
(though given what our dark day does portray,
    it seems the state preferred).

If you feel you've lost your way and judge the other lost,
walk in dark Gethsemane's hour before your time is done.
    For beyond the day of dire torment,
when it seems all hope is gone, we find a gardener working—
    redemption's Easter Son.

Disturbing Definitions

There are those frequent inconvenient
boys and girls—men and women
who don't fit the image we promote.

You are disabled or blind or deaf, and
you might well twitch or jerk about,
muttering sounds that make you strange
or staring in icy silence from unfocused eyes.
You may be too feminine or masculine
to fit the sexual roles we so tightly have defined.
Too tall, too short, too fat
    (seems one can never be too thin),
too humped or bumped or scarred—
you are people, who by the fates are real,
who we too willingly discard, ignore, or bully.
And while you need our tender love
and to be seen by us as real, we instead, too often,
walk right by, as though you were only shadows.

The Gospel According to Huck Finn

"I was a-trembling, because I had to decide, forever, betwixt two thing, and I knowed it. I studied a minute, sorta of holding my breath, and then I says to myself, "All right, then, I'll go to hell.'"
~Huck Finn from *The Adventures of Huckleberry Finn* by Mark Twain

    It would seem the Texas State Board of Education (May 2010) finds certain words and phrases highly suspect and, where possible, is casting them out of state-approved textbooks. Among these are *justice* and the *common good*. As a Christian, knowing that this is being done to preserve some moral imperative to mitigate humanistic influences gives me pause as to how much longer I can call myself a Christian.
    It is not without a wide latitude of tolerance that I have comfortably acknowledged that my story is a Christian story. It is the native language in which my history is framed—it is the very context of my life. I offer a latitude of tolerance, for example, for the Biblical inerrancy believers, who, by my most compassionate embrace, it seems to me, must simply ignore huge portions of scripture. That this is justified not in overlooking them, but through their "correct interpretation," reminds me too much of a politician putting forward pitiful plausible deniability claims. I wouldn't mind such dogmatic adherence were it not for the too frequent espousal of the portions of the Bible that justify their prejudice and hatred, at the expense of the words of the sermon on the Mount or John's admonition that one who says they love God while hating their brother is a liar.
    Lest I come off too harsh regarding the fundamentalists, let me be clear that a broad liberal interpretation of Scripture hasn't exactly brought about peace on Earth, either. And in the Episcopal Church, of which I have been a member for nearly thirty years, I am less and less comfortable with miter, chasuble, ordination, and Church cannon—even though I sat

on the Diocesan Standing Committee, which evaluates ordinands for the Bishop's final say.

I have been a close enough observer of several denominations, including Mennonite, Church of God (Anderson), Methodist, Catholic, and Anglican, to name a few, that I can describe pretty accurately what each would list as the precepts for salvation. Yet I find myself in the same place as Huck Finn when he had to make the "moral" decision about whether to give up Jim as a runaway slave or break the law and honor a friendship. All right, then, Huck, I'll go to hell, too, for I can no longer respect the "authority" of christianity (small "c" intentional), for it has too long perpetuated its bankrupt voice in the name of moral authority. Save for the small remnants of its history in which it has fed the hungry, clothed the naked, defended the persecuted, and died working for justice for the poor, the Church has been largely about institutional staying power. Even the smallest denominations or nondenominational churches control the "message" of the Church, which revolves around how their group interprets "key" passages of Scripture.

Scripture did not start with Genesis 1:1. John suggests an answer to its true origin: "In the beginning was the Word, and the Word was with God and the Word was God." Scripture did not end with Revelation. Between Genesis and Revelation, there is a rich history of fact, myth, and parable, and none of us can prove which is which. It is, as they say, all true, and some of it actually happened. The very fact that Jesus teaches in parables more than with historical, biblical examples perhaps ought to suggest to us that the moral imperative is the lesson—not the chapter and verse in which it is found. Even when Jesus quotes scripture, he fails in the chapter-and-verse crowd because he rarely quotes the direct source of his teaching. On multiple occasions, he actually teaches, "You have heard it said... but I say." It is in this way, he directly addresses "eye for an eye" retaliation, which, though he refuted it as a doctrine 2,000 years ago, the Church continues to support in complacent sympathy with military and criminal justice retribution and retaliation.

The institutional Church did a great disservice to the gifts of the Holy Spirit by canonizing scripture without adding to that canon over the millennia. The Church has been a poor guide for the faithful in understanding the ways in which God speaks. We have not allowed richness in thought and connection to our elemental creation to be an integral part of our Christian experience.

Perhaps we should reflect on the testimony against the Church, were it to come before an international criminal court, charged with crimes against humanity, obstruction of justice, and criminal facilitation. Having too often turned a blind eye to injustice in economic exploitation, military action, and prejudice of every kind, what might our defense be? We were too distracted by arguments over orthodoxy, doctrine, and inerrancy of scripture? May God have mercy on us.

Zero Sum Game

I don't know, with any precision, how
    the Earth is warming, cooling,
or staying about the same. The climate changes with a
constancy that leaves us humbled by its power.

But whatever our effect may be
    upon a change at large,
I would think by now that we'd be just plain tired
    of polluting what's in our charge.

Closure of Pain

If I close my eyes to beauty,
if I close my hands to care,
if I close my heart to hope,
    it's easy enough to flee
the very things that God has put in front of me.

Grief's Work

When the loved so close are dying,
the world needs people like us.
Our grief is real, but it doesn't show.
It's for us to handle the details of woe.
And that's okay. For us, it's closure—
brought to fruition by composure.

The Walk
(A reflection on the movie *The Snow Walker*)

The native mind might well describe
an afterlife as Earth itself, with
    good hunting, tall grass,
    and flowing streams.

The Christian mind relegates the
    Earth as early hell,
while dreaming of otherworldly streets of gold
and doors of pearl. It's odd, it seems to me,
to want the glitter of wealth's allure instead
of nature's beauty for a world so marvelously divine.

We've not found our home here
    for reasons that don't compute,
except perhaps that we wander too swiftly
    past the flowers and the trees.
Ever seeking more control and the trappings
it affords, we miss the beauty and
    the grace of walking well.

Contemplation's Fruit

After prayer and contemplation
judging you becomes a task,
    as the faults you hold
seem less your own to claim. You are
mean and think you're clever,
but who am I for such endeavors?
Splitting hairs between your sad sins
    and the measure of my own.
If the Way has taught us not to judge,
perhaps I'd better heed the warning,
for as sure as I can see,
    you might as well be me.

Computation

As our relationship to computers
has grown from bewilderment to
    fascination and obsession,
we have taken on most unhealthy habits.
    Analogies of computer-speak as
human function is a diminution of our sacred core.
The CPU is not a brain, and it has no heart to love.
    Its OS is just programmed commands that
know no sense of awe. It generates data in volumes,
    without wisdom's guiding way.

Some say the computer has changed our world, but
such change is in function, not in form.
It hasn't changed our hate for enemies
or our contempt for land and air. On the
things that really matter, like all machines before it,
    a computer is much more hype than hope.
In the end, it's just a tool to use or misuse as you please. The
net effect of all its work remains poorly understood.
Perhaps we're afraid of what we'd find if we knew
    the bad outweighed the good.

My Moodiness

    Melancholy
follows me hand in hand each and every day.
That may sound rather pitiful to some,
and big pharma is glad to profit if they can.
    But no pill for me is needed.
I have the counter of pure joy as well.
That my day meanders between the two
is quite okay by me. My melancholy keeps
me from attaching to giddy optimism's scam,
    which supplants hope's noble cause,
while my joy pulls melancholy back
    to hope beyond myself.

    Some know true depression—the
most repressive weight there is. I do not confuse
my ever-swinging moods for the burden that they bear,
    nor do I know the fix.
All I can do is have the humility to see
    how easily it could be me.

Love in Question

Have I ever loved? For a fragment
    here and there.
But as a force that guides my day
I've done little to let it sway my way.

I am not alone, though it would be
    better if I were. Some paths
should be overgrown, but love's path is,
    and it should not be.

Tyranny
(Reflecting on the news of presidential kill lists and the whistleblower investigation into their unintended disclosure to the public, June 2012)

It seems clear by now that executive power cannot resist
    overstepping good for evil's
    tempting ways—
    whether monarch, dictator, or president.
Let us find another way besides the arrogance of power.
Follow the Swiss and rid us of the imperial presidency.
One person cannot solve our problems and
    one man (or woman)
    should never rule the world.
This is not democracy—even if for a term.
    It is power's oldest lie.
    It is tyranny we can't deny.

Claims

There are few things that I claim to be
and many that I don't. I'm not an inventor,
counselor, or priest—nor a teacher, artist,
or musician. Not a doctor or lawyer, statesman or other
noble role. I'm not an intellectual—not even all that bright.
    My credentials are unimpressive,
regardless of the jobs you recite.
I've never been sure of vocation,
while other's pronounce God's call.

I do claim to have some patience
where others' fuses run short.
I am the jack of a few useful trades,
yet certainly master of none.
I'm troubled enough to write my thoughts,
whether anyone reads them or not.
And that's about all I can claim, with one notable exception.
    My life has been extraordinary
    from the moment of its inception.

Elegy to Laura (Viator) Gardener (1928–2012)

There was a woman,
so small and frail,
it seemed life's difficulties
would make her fail.
There was a woman whose
quiet way,
may have seemed to others
her reason to stay.
There was a woman whose
long contented years
might have looked simple,
but they were not without fears.
We called her wife, sister,
mother, and friend.
She rests now with Christ
in her calm peaceful end.
Her strength shall stay with us,
her laughter and smile;
Her prayers for her loved ones
with us all the while.

Purchased Votes

We say that we are appalled at the big money
spent on our political campaigns, but you and I
keep right on rewarding the biggest spenders
by electing the greedy scoundrels again and again.

It is said, in ninety-four percent of elections,
the one who spent the most takes the day.
That says more about our gullibility to marketing ploys
than our devotion to the work of democracy.

The real work of democracy is informed consent.
Allowing pundits and PACs to do the thinking
for us is not informed consent. Anyway, there's no
proof that pundits and PACs are pondering noble good.

Dare to disagree without being disagreeable. Your
way might be right, or there may be a better way. If
your loyalty lies with party over justice and compassion,
then the hateful, vitriolic, mistrustful way remains.

Trinity as Concept

The trinity is not a stumbling block to my reason.
That is not to say that the Church has done
such an extraordinary job at addressing
    the theology of the trinity
or that the Nicene and Apostles' creed spell it out
so succinctly as to offer me such certitude.
No, my view of the trinity is not certitude over mystery,
    but rather faith in the cosmic mystery.

We have a cosmos of billions of galaxies, trillions of stars,
and an unknown number of planets.
There is the mysterious foundation of it all.
We might well call this foundation Father (and Mother),
    for lack of a more understandable term.
We also call it Love, for we would do well
to heed the prophetic notion that God indeed is love.
We, and all creation, have been loved into being.

We have our actual existence on this one planet—
    the living things of this Earth that,
through the logos of God—the Word as flesh among us—
we see made manifest in history as Jesus,
    the Jewish carpenter.
That such enfleshment may come to us,
in other times of history in other ways,
    I believe to be possible, if not
    altogether probable.
We need this interactive heartbeat,
not just like our own, metaphorically, but
that is indeed our very own, to place
the incomprehensible expanse of the universe
    in human terms.
How else can we translate cosmic love into

    our human dimension?
We have this ethereal Spirit, which moves
throughout time and space, within and beyond
    understandable dimensions.
We sense an otherworldly quality
    within us,
    between us, and beyond us,
that cannot be explained away, even
by the most rational, scientific mind. It can be dismissed
or ignored, but it remains there to confound and challenge
    our all-knowing arrogance.

I would not stone the heathen who suggests there is no God,
    though the limits to their reason
    requires its own leap of faith.
Nor would I burn the heretic who might suggest
additional dimensions of God. Yet
as the trinitarian nature of God seems to have been present
    with the psalmist and the prophets,
so am I quite content to let it rest there in the finite knowledge
we possess of a seemingly infinite creation.
    Creator, Incarnate Word, Spirit—
    in unity as one day we may be.

What May Be

At what point do we decide
whether we love the world enough
to assume responsibility for it?
That, is what the good shepherd does—
even if it means laying down his life
    for love of the sheep.
It is awakening to the fact that
what we do on and to the Earth and its creatures,
    the Earth takes on in permanence.
When we forfeit our divinely given gifts of imagination,
we fall prey to the great disease of our perilous time.
We can only see life
    as it must be
    as defined by the dualistic
    and closed-up mind.
We become cruel shepherds. We lead
our brothers and sisters dumb before the slaughter.
Or, at best, we allow cruel shepherds to lead for us.

It is this image of one way that must be,
instead of the many ways that may be,
that leads to the ovens of Auschwitz; to the
    exploitation of all creation;
to the drones droning night and day over remote villages
    in faraway lands and on our borders;
to violence, as the only way to an illusory security
    of the small mind.

There are the ways that may be, but they
require us to use our divinely given imagination,
    whose eyes will always see
all the different ways that life may be.

Journey

Ours is a journey from darkness to light.
It's a life's work, which does not come easily
    or automatically.
Whatever gifts and graces come to us as
we make that journey—that which is both
    means and end—
bring order to the chaos of our lives.

We must press on with the work
of striving toward a better moral understanding,
    attainable through
    the wisdom of creation.
And if the journey's troubles wake us in the night,
pondering the darkness and the light,
may we find ourselves holding each pilgrim's walk in prayer,
    for together, we must
    make the journey
    toward Love's eternal light.

Church as Concept

May the Church doors of our land fling open to the world,
welcoming all without condition.
We shall be merciful, for then we shall know
    the peace of Christ, and
Christ's peace is our offering to this fractured, broken world.

There are dirty feet in our cities. Let us wash them.
There are multitudes staring at two fish and a loaf of bread,
    awaiting our blessing. Let us feed them.
There are enemies who fear us. Let us love them.
There are people imprisoned by injustice. Let us free them.
There are poor who see no hope. Let us lift them.
There are throngs lost in addiction. Let us heal them.
There are weakened and lost wanderers.
    Let us lead them.
There are sheep the Church has driven away.
    Let us search for them.
There are those who have been judged.
    Let us embrace them.
There are those who have been hurtful. Let us forgive them.

Let us seek the humility that knows
    that none, ordained or unordained,
    holds truth or wisdom
    securely in their palm.
It is a pilgrim's journey that cannot be made in
    isolation from Love's mystery.

Elegy to Gary Oyer (1956–1975)

You've been dead for nearly forty years—
    far longer than I ever knew you—
    far longer than you ever lived.
Your death, though not the first in my
experience, remained with me every day
for years. One day, I realized that the
day before had passed without any thought of you,
yet you had come again into my mind.
    Your terrible death
was and is a hard thing to forget, but my
memories, all those days of all these years,
were of your life and not your death.
Together we went to Church, to band,
to 4-H, to Company, and to the hay fields.
I still recall your energetic ways and
    the grief your early death left
    for mother, father,
    siblings, friends, and
    neighbor boys like me.

Vision Without Blinders

Equality, my dear brothers and sisters,
is not treating everyone the same. Equality
is seeing the very essence of human dignity
in each and every person, and finding and honoring
    their gifts and graces.
And finding and honoring our own.

In all Deference to Jefferson

In all deference to the semantical genius of Jefferson,
    the notion that Americans can pursue
happiness as some grabbable commodity or prize has not
served us well. We have the pursuit and grabbing
down well enough. But just when we think we've reached it,
our eye catches the flashes of a yet further shining—
foils of pursuit. Happiness and bliss are given freely and
are known most often when no pursuit is underway.

For those with minds to observe and those with hearts to feel,
happiness and bliss are the context of creation,
    as its essence, and there is
    nothing to pursue.

Quarrelsome

Perhaps unlike my mother,
your mother didn't teach you
not to be quarrelsome, and
you missed the lesson from others
    along the way. Well, too bad for us,
as you think it now a virtue—
your skills a wonder to behold. But it is not
a virtue or a skill. And the only wonder
    is its ongoing, sad assertion of your will.

What We Instill

How easily we instill
our prejudice and fears.
Children hear the hate.
They see the condescension.
And from the jokes and pokes,
they amplify intentions.

They bully and they sneer.
They call out names and
instill fear. They gesture
with finger, fist, and hateful eye.
They paint and scribble epithets
on windows, walls, and lockers doors.

With basic training over, they
leave the schoolhouse grounds
taking the tolerated "pranks
of misspent youth" along as
lessons learned, and pride and
ego keep the cycle going.

But all this can end on a
dime. It takes no curricular
funding or special education.
It only takes the family's heart
to see that without love for all,
    we are not free.

Red and Blue

I have seen the images from space.
There are no red states or blue states—
    mostly shades of brown and green.
In fact, except for rivers' and lakes' contributions to the map,
one can't tell where one state starts
    and another finds its end.
Our infantile, polarizing, color-coded schemes
are tiresome and misleading—serving only
    to endorse propaganda's cynical claim.
I am not red, nor am I blue. And
    last I looked, neither were you.
So, let's end this state of coloring states
for the sake of our country's ultimate fate.

Point of Our Play

We start mighty early teaching young minds
that there are winners and losers, and nothing in between.
The winners are heroes with fame and big cars;
the losers are useless—not part of our scene.
Our coliseums and boardrooms
    are filled with allure,
as life's ultimate prize that pride keeps alive.
Pride's control is the original sin of the game,
and the game takes no prisoners and fosters no friends—
    it is willing to expend all to win.
The escalating madness of takeovers and wars insists
that their winning will be good for us all. But winning
is shallow and dies in the light, lacking its root in
    goodness and truth.
Our obsession with winning has sacrificed much,
when in camaraderie's grace we could find true accord.
When in tune with our place and the world we call home,
    the great need for winning
    becomes pointless and dull.

    Can we imagine a time when
play is just play, and not the game of superior ranking?
The key, as we see, is indeed to *imagine*.
Imagine a world where shared laughter and smiles
    are the point and the reward,
with no need for ranking or gathering spoils.
Imagine together the reality of souls—
    playful and joyful all our years.

Digging

John-Marie Preston said to me that she could
always tell when a man's hands had been in
the dirt. She believed that the farmer's, rancher's,
and gardener's connection to the earth brought
wisdom not conferred by any degree. She also
believed that a dog should be permitted to dig holes
in the backyard. Thus, I learned two bits
of wisdom from her, which may have been
my first true actualizations of contemplation.

Checks and Balances

Some would contend that our system
of political checks and balances isn't
working very well, but they are clearly wrong.
The checks are pouring in, and the balance
in payments received balance as closely as ever
    with the favors granted.

None of the Above

Your ubiquitous polls,
    used and misused,
present the prescribed questions and statements
with your set list of defined answers. You
need such narrow conformity to fit your
    computer data trending
and to assert your self-perceived importance.
But people don't trend as neatly
as computers and news graphics demand.
    You prefer narrowing
the choices to best reflect your own agenda.
What scenario doesn't have
    a hundred,
    a thousand,
    ten thousand opinions?
Yet you squeeze opinion down to the few
same lame and old, tired responses.

You shall know the data
and the data shall keep us captive.
The freedom of truth lies in the millions of
complex and changing minds
    your poll can never capture.

Dull Perception

I hope that at some overdone cocktail party,
where there is someone who thinks they know me,
I am never described as clever.
Somehow, the general description,
which is supposed to be high praise
from the giver, is too often an endorsement
of like to like:
    the cynical of the cynical,
    the arrogant of the arrogant,
    the condescending of the condescending.
And the one proclaiming another's cleverness
works from the assumed social position
of being one *so* clever as to discern
    another's cleverness and thus proclaim
their self-asserted place in the circle of the clever.
    But such is not cleverness.
Dull perception of a small, contracted mind
is what it is. Like an old wine gone to
vinegar yet still cherished as some
great vintage, so the mind of these serve
    their bitter gall.
The world does not grow kinder from cynicism's host.
The humble men and women who mark
our world with peace and grace don't make it
onto the list of cocktail party admiration.
Yet it is the likes of these who stand
    for our best hope.
They who walk, wakefully, in ignorance
    and know it.

Mount Dora, FL, 2013–2015

On a line from Barbara Douglas

The path of life is sold to us as a logical progression.
The maturity of our decisions
    (so the marketing hype insists)
brings with it the comfort and security in which
    a pursuit of happiness
is said to be found. Yet life is not
    logical progression, and the measure
of our maturity might well bring us to the absurdity
or tragedy of the moment, when at some moment, you know
    that life as planned
    is to be life unplanned.
We move into the unconscious epiphany—
a clarity—as we "abandon the rational mind"
and enter mystery's incarnation with unpredicted
    joy and tears,
    singing and silence,
    hope and fear.
We move and are moved.
    We reach to death and love,
    and we live again.

Bound

The Christ eternally speaks to love and
its eternal offering of the bewildering notion—
    knowing the truth
    shall set us free.

Lost, and not free, our quest has sent us
out looking for an antichrist who
    will be the sign of the end of
time—rapture waiting in the wings.

We love to label the evil that is
another's—masking as it does our own.
But the antichrists are speaking always and
bear no power to set the end of time,
though they move always toward destruction.
And they are not known in one face or nation, but in
the ubiquitous face of pride and greed and hate.

The bewildering line of Christ is seen, in the
    clearest light,
when the unspoken truth of antichrists
are heard. "You shall embrace the lie,
    and the lie shall keep you bound."

Violence in the Night

What is this bondage? I don't want these
dreams. The betrayal they demand
is damning to the core—casting the soul to
an inner darkness that haunts me in the night.
In my dreams, no matter how peaceable I
want to be, the gun in hand fires my
bloody submission into the lie, but it never dies.
    It will not die.
    It cannot die.
It reaches with its hateful grasp toward me,
and I fire hopelessly again into the undying antichrist,
whose weapon of hate now betrays me.
    This answer to my peace betrays me.

Mercifully, truth awakens me. And as the mind
eases its way out of the blood and fear
and back into the Christ, the lie vanishes,
    as all lies must, in truth.
And grace reminds me yet again: The dream
was real. We cannot kill our way to peace.
Violence, a futile act, brings no relief.
We cannot kill our way to peace. And no
matter how the lie may pursue me, I always
    awaken to truth and am free.
Only love will find our way to peace.

Presumption
(A reflection on Bob Corker's quote regarding the 2013 national security proposals on border security and the charge of treason for Edward Snowden)

    "We are doing something great,"
the greatest nation in the world.
If you don't think so, pay attention to the press!
Our "free market" drives the markets of
the world for good (or ill), and our CAFOs
    yield the most efficient meat (if not humanely).

Our mega-christianity is as inerrant
as the holy book through which we pick and
choose our way to pious pride (while turning a blind eye).
The unyielding might on which we stand secure
    now encompasses the globe,
down to our data streams of mega-bits and bytes
 (peace and privacy lost relics of distant dreams).

We shall keep our borders tight so that
    waifs don't wander in (and
    see the dream betrayed by all the lies).
Our greatness is assured at every turn
    by (purchased) powers,
who cry aloud their great and faulty assertion—
    "We are doing something great!"
Be clear, you, "we," who presume
    to speak for everyone.
You do not speak for me.

Turn Our Eyes from Ourselves

Lost in a world of urban sophistication,
the passing cars, with their occupancy
rate that rarely exceeds one, far surpass
any pedestrian movement. Yet even when
on the sidewalk with fellow passing sophisticates,
not so much as a nod of the head or muttered
     hello passes between us.
One oversized man, with a stack of flyers, does
look me in the eye and wants to know if Jesus is my
personal savior. I'm too slow to respond that
     I take him as the Savior of all, so that
should cover me; instead, I offer the evangelical
affirmative, so that I may be on my way in the
hot San Antonio sun. The reflected heat from all
the concrete offers less solace to me than the
filtered light through the live oaks and Spanish moss
of home. Bonhoeffer was right, we turned from
the witness of the Gospel to the witness of our piety.
     "For goodness sake, let's turn
     our eyes from ourselves!"
And so I turn my eyes back to the world of urban
sophistication I've been dropped into for these few days
by a roaring 757, having cut its way
     through thick, gray-green air.
     (I instinctively hack for a few seconds.)
The biggest, least modest building on Santa Rosa
is Texas DPS, which could house several Swiss villages,
though not with any measure of the same grace.
     (Smaller government for Texans.)
Across the street, half a mile of something recently
demolished. Progress is coming again—however
temporal its existence may be. Along the *mercado*,
I pass a (mercifully) forgotten grade of tacky wares
that I can't quite figure out. What is the redeeming

value here? I study them. Look deeply for some better
perspective. There is none. Ugliness for sale.
    Cheap but expensive—
        to the consumer and to the world.
I feel all the urban and none of the sophistication.
My quiet hotel room seems the better alternative, and
so I enter my three-day hermitage and hope for
    some divine light
on how to bear witness to the Gospel
    for even such as these—another generation,
    lost at the Alamo.

Culpability

There is no more plausible deniability. Barnacles of
culpability cling tightly on hardened layered shells,
made thick from our insatiable diet of lies
    touting our own greatness.
Democracy in shambles, we must bear the cost and
stop the indifference, to care about what the
bending arch of justice will one day demand.
    Stripping us of deniability,
    stripping us of condescension,
we shall lie before the world exposed, our shells
    cracked open, our flesh as vulnerable and weak
as those we now so arrogantly detest.

A Prophet's Pondering Way

Would that we could ponder. We are the great
generation of information, data—even knowledge.
But we are thoughtless—easily stirred by emotion,
    be it laughter, rage, or tears.
Emotion does not carry us from knowledge to
deepest wisdom. Such depth requires
    the prophet's pondering way.
Never do you see the prophet's words
    go viral in our cyber-ruling age.
There's no gratification instant enough
in searching deep within, and so we chow down
on the empty calories of empty facts and empty words.
    We've outsourced thought to pundits
in a very shabby deal. Polluted rhetoric that chokes
    the throat of truth. Oh,
would that we could ponder as Mary did in quiet ways.
    Cable news or wisdom. You decide.

Image

The image handlers have it all laid out by role.

Must look presidential: power-suit equal to or better than
the Wall Street bankers to whom you are beholden.
    (When in doubt, quote Jefferson or Lincoln.)

Must look holy: silken brocade miter
and crafted Crozier to keep the sheep gazing from the pew.
    (Walk softly but carry a big stick.)

Must look famous: dark glasses, exotic hair,
designer clothes, designer teeth, designer homes,
designer lives (if a bit flawed), thus assuring adoring fans.

We've even allowed the great Jesus tragedy, with its
    crown of thorns,
    a cruel cross,
    and bloody death,
to be some painless image for our stained-glass windows.
But such a death as this is not a frozen image in time;
it is torture's ongoing quest to kill love in all its forms.

Can we let go of image? Can we love ourselves that much?
    Image is bartered, manipulated, stipulated.
    Love is essence. Essence is love,
always given manipulation and stipulation free.

Intertwined

The clever (to the apparently not so clever) ask,
    "Do you have a mind of your own?"
(Only the clever can state an absolute affirmative.)
Answer simply, "No" (as humility knows truth).

Your mind is a patchwork. Whose lives and words
are being pieced together there? Are they colorful,
diverse, and richly textured? What scraps
and patterns are you stitching there?
    Who are your companions in the work?
Are you quilting it with care and grace?
Will it warm your children's children and
    endure in lasting beauty?

Or like all that is ugliness,
prove not worth the effort, fray, and be tossed,
with no regard for what might have been?

For Desmond Tutu
("I would refuse to go to a homophobic heaven. No, I would say sorry, I mean I would much rather go to the other place. I would not worship a God who is homophobic and that is how deeply I feel about this." Arch Bishop Desmond Tutu at the Free and Equal Campaign in Cape Town, July 2013)

Once I thought of you as more
    simpleton than saint, but that
was before the work of contemplation
had pierced my heart. I can see that
you are real and how illusory are those
who dismiss you out of hand.
Now, like Huck, you say,
    "All right then, I'll go to hell."
You will not bow to God made small.
You are both simple and saint in
the great divinity of love,
    with Grace for all. With a face
and laugh and voice made pure by tears of joy and
years of pain, you are beauty to the core.
Your God is great. Your God is good.
Your God is big enough for all. Hell
could never hold you, though sinful ones
would send you there just for being kind.
Blessed are you, pure in heart. You have seen
    the God so many can't.
Blessed are you, peacemaker. Indeed,
    you are God's child.
Blessed are you, persecuted one.
    Heaven, not Hell, is yours.

Shaken and Stirred

What degree of fine are you? Our culture
asks the question as to how our day or mood
or health in frequency is trending. No time
for deep analysis. Respond, "I'm fine," if you please.
    It may be close enough to truth
    to send us on our merry way.

There are more days than not when what is,
is fine enough. I'll not press you for a deeper meaning
on such days. I'll leave you to deal with darkness
and your mood without my help. Though unspoken,
I seem to hear you say,
    "I'm fine, dammit!
    Leave well enough alone."

On those days when you are not, and you need
a patient ear, grab my shoulder, shake me,
stir me to respond. Sometimes the darkness
is too deep to face it alone, the fear and its confusion.
    "I am not fine, dammit!
    Can't you see? I cannot be alone."

Yesterday's sins and sorrows may haunt us
all our years. But they are not the
present grace offered freely for our days.
What might your tomorrow bring if you
see another dawn? Be shaken by the mercy—
    stirred by the compassion.
The darkest days have passed because
    a friend
        had time to spare.

Snippet

Riding in the cab at dark-thirty. Headed
to the airport—heading home. While most
of the world around me and the quiet cabby
remains dark and asleep, sucking kilowatts,
    the billboards light the desecrated way
    of 24/7 commercialism.
I notice only one. In huge letters it reads,
    "The land of more."

What it certainly lacks in grace it
does, I decide, afford in honesty
about whatever it was that I
was supposed to be wanting in this
    land of more.

It doesn't really matter that I missed the product.
The subliminal programming code has
been uploaded. One viral snippet of code—
    the land of more.

So many things in life I want less of
in this land of more. Billboards, for one.

Gradualism
(A reflection on the statistical findings that birth defects in parts of Iraq, from depleted uranium bombs, are fourteen times more frequent than following Hiroshima and Nagasaki, and on the militarization of the US–Mexico border)

There is an odd phenomenon in the fast pace of
the global-hubris-armament economy. It is
absolutely dependent on gradualism.
Things have to creep in so that we can come to
the great standstill-ism of the people
    that empire must have
    to wield its expanding evil.

With apathy and distraction firmly rooted,
we no longer care about the details that we
might abhor if we were moving toward peace,
which is, necessarily, also moving away in the
    aftermath of our deeds.
The appalling birth defects, poisoned water,
    blasted homes and roads and dams
that lie in the wake of our wonted destruction.

Building walls to keep more out and prisons to
keep more in. Bursting bubbles so the rich can
enrich their portfolio with the bailout, forged
in debt for some unsuspecting generation to come.
    Subsidizing mega-Walmart
through food stamps and Medicaid for workers
    who cannot earn a living wage.
Good capitalists and their political minions
finally finding admiration for communist leaders
who have proven that they know better than we do
how to get people to work for nothing.

We've stood still in inattention long enough. It is

time (as the Shaker way) to turn, turn,
till by turning, turning, we come 'round right.

Turn, then, wherever you may be.
We must no longer stand in dazed denial
of the injustice of our history and our days.
The suffering children cry for a better destiny.
    It is ours to give.
    It is ours to deny.

Momma Said

Like so many kids today, our two dogs never did
know their hit-and-run daddy. But they sure got
    a heavy dose of momma.
"Momma said beware of unfixed boys."

We can't quite tell what they are. We try things out.
    Deux chiens. Zwei Hunde. Dos perros.
Whatever we call them, it evokes the same look.
Either they are multilingual or they just
think we don't speak dog. Verbal communications
have little point, it would seem. Even the little yappin'
dog next door, they pretty much ignore.

"Pointless chatter!" one says to the other.

(They don't know it, but both masters are
fluent in dog. Don't tell them.)

"At least when we growl, there is something
to growl at. Shut that damn dog up,"
the other mutters in her sleepy, curmudgeonly voice.

"Momma said, 'If you ain't got somethin' worth
sayin', keep quiet.'"

They do like to hear a few things from us
in our native tongue—protein and exercise
items top the list. *Meat. Cheese. Walk.*
    Dogs go outside?
"Momma said, 'Stare at them pathetically to get action.'"

And they have a few things they don't like:
Get down! Quit! I'm petted out!

"Momma said, 'Ignore what you don't like,'"

About some things, they are remarkably selective.
They can discern the best rugs, the best pillows,
the best potential hand for petting. Anything
     black looks better with dog hair.
     Doing business in the yard.
"Momma said, 'Sniff out just the right spot.'"

They are much more perceptive than we.
Any noise out of the routine may be a biddy-gitter.
     Beware!
"Momma said, 'There's no good garbage truck.'"

The instant something on their list of favorite foods
comes out of the icebox, they are there with
gratitude for what they are about to receive.
"Momma said, 'If there aren't
     jackrabbits, bologna will do.'"

Indeed, they know that persistence and hope
     are the keys
     to life well lived.
And I know you won't believe it, but they know
that persistence and hope are two very different
     realms of consciousness.
"Momma said, 'People don't know how to just be.'"

For all our fussin' at the hair and the nudgin' and
the pawin' and the lickin', they still seem to think
     we're okay.
We don't know why. More than we deserve.
"Momma said, 'These two aren't the best,
but don't be too picky.'"
     Unfailing kindness for imperfect masters.

Canines carrying on generational fidelity in
    unconditional friendship, just like Momma said.

A Stand for Love of Country

I do not pledge allegiance to the flag
or to the empire for which it stands.
One global oppressor, consumed with greed,
    always dividing,
with "liberty" and "justice" for sale.

Fantasism

I don't have anything against fantasy.
Served me pretty well in childhood. Serves
me well now, when I want to take my mind
    to what could be.
But really! Does it belong in the national
discourse as a measure of success?

Economic wellbeing as measured by profits to
shareholders and the value of inflated stock options.
    Fantasy.

National security as measured by secrecy
and military and para-military police control.
    Fantasy.

Health as measured by the treatment of disease
and the money spent on medical care.
    Fantasy.

Education as measured by standardized testing;
STEM as superior to the humanities and arts.
    Fantasy.

The optimism of fantasism. Hopeless for
the helpless. Lifeblood of the lie.

What Lives Become

That tangent moment, so long past, seems now
as distant and unfamiliar as our separate lives
have become. Your life in one context and
mine estranged from it, and you from me. No
animosity. No pain. No regret. Just different lives,
in different places, with different friends and faces.

Your life urbane and mine pastoral. Whatever
griefs or joys you have known these decades past,
you've shared with others and not with me. So it
has been for my years, too. Affection only some remote
and detached sentiment. Still present. An inexplicable
connection that may be imagined or real.

One certainty, which must be said in gratitude:
I was forever changed. Made comfortable in my own
skin by you. Suddenly awake to love for what it could
offer to someone else. That the final someone was,
indeed, someone else is the reality of seeking what we
don't know is ours until fidelity is given a chance to root.

No chartered course can ever take us again to that time
when the arc of your young life came assuredly toward
me in love's embrace. The moment is spent and gone.
Its worth remains luminous yet oddly cold. It is cherished
and neglected. It is, in the end, what lives become when
two strong wills and youthful passions pass in the night.

In Flight

Settled, but not, into the Delta 757. I ask
the corporate-programmed, smiling
attendant if she can turn down
the blaring preflight, maddening
muzak. She assures me,
    yes, she can.
It is, as it happens, a statement
of her professed capability,
but not her willingness. The
volume remains unchanged.
Impossible to block out.

My furrowed brow has no impact
on her resolve or her smile. My mood
turns foul because of the brow,
    the muzak,
    or most likely both.

The strident nails-on-chalkboard,
nasal soprano being broadcast is
trying to sell me and the crowd,
in which no one is really listening, the idea
that in living our lives there are no mistakes.

I beg to differ.

(Taking a job that requires
frequent flying comes to mind.)

And Wisdom begs to differ as well.
Long called sin, the violence,
destruction, and exploitation the
prophets have named as
    our mistakes to own

are not some simple challenge to
the journey, as she assures me
on and on—chorus after chorus.

(Like bad jazz improv and some
operatic arias that don't know
when enough is enough, I wonder
when she will make an end.)

Our lives are the essence of choice.
We choose love, humility, wholeness, or
we choose a life of mistakes. We can
be challenged to move beyond
our mistakes, but not if we choose
  to pretend we've made none.

(I have a brother who I've never heard
own a mistake, despite the evidence—
ex-wives—to the contrary.)

Carrying on the reckless tradition of
  "I did it my way,"
we wander aimlessly on a journey
with no destination. Oblivious to
the regrets we should have had for
not paying attention along the
  Jericho road, with its wrecked lives
  of generational mistakes
that we continue to make. Before
redemption can heal us, we must fess up.

The brainwashing, bad muzak
heralds in dissonance and decibels
  its continued assault.
After a brief audio respite,
mandatory for takeoff, it's back on.

This time, an inflight eBay ad informs me
that I have entered the shop-i-sphere. I can
shift my focus from the bad soprano
to shopping (in the land of more).

Their mistake. We're above ten thousand feet.
    I put on my technology
    to override their technology.
I hit shuffle and hear the more glorious
tones of Libera. The pure voices of
non-strident boy sopranos—
England's purest gift to the world.

The sounds immediately begin doing
the work of neutralizing
    the muzak
    from the psyche!

I stare out the window at the
Georgia countryside below. The boys
assure me, as though the Gentle Spirit
had perfectly queued them to my present
    state of mind and place,

Deep peace of the flowing air to you.
Deep peace of the quiet earth to you.
Deep peace of Christ to you.

Remarkable! From momentary
madness to simple tears of grace
and overwhelming joy.
    Resonance of the divine.
Deep peace flowing with me through the air.
    Deep peace, mistakes and all.

While I'm in San Diego, I think

that I shall gaze out onto the ocean.
Deep peace of the running wave. And
on my red-eye, Saturday night return home,
    I shall ponder
    the deep peace of the gentle night;
    the deep peace of the shining stars.

Posing Questions

            i.

It is really quite astounding. I have no
children. I could easily enough live
out my life with the assurance that I will
make it to my end without having to bother
with any of the real problems of the world.
Live obliviously and die. History's history.
    But I do care.
It occupies my mind in the day and in
the night. It challenges the very hope
    I cling to.

It is astounding how so many I know,
while carrying on about grandchildren,
seem to exhibit no care whatsoever.

When challenged on one point, for bearing
false witness in their perpetuation of the micro-second
ubiquitous transport of Internet lies, I was told,
    "And anyway, I don't really care."
Sadly, obvious. Though truly
astounding. To know it and to be proud of it.

(Pride doth proceed destruction. Maximum force,
relentlessly applied.)

When will we care for the innocence of
    generations yet unborn?
That is the high calling. Death to self
made small through pride's control.
    The promise of life eternal—not as some
divine future existence of self, but as a participatory
act of creation in which we are the voice.
    The gift of love for the least yet to be.

We've not done well in caring for the least
who are already here. Might we find our own
transformation if we could imagine caring
for the least yet to be? And if so,
     when shall we agree to begin? When?

           ii.
Over the years, we have quickly evolved
    taller in body;
stature of character unchanged or shrinking.
Might we ever allow the latter to catch up
with the former? Or, having squandered
standing taller for so long, when will
the Just-Judge cast us,
     the deceivers—the deceived,
on our long and flabby bellies, to crawl for eternity
in the dust of our destruction?

           iii.
As the news reports go, a celebrity earned
$77,000,000 in one year; the hedge fund CEO
more than $200,000,000. Earned? Really?
     Love's labor lost
for zeros and commas after a dollar sign.

Mistaken Identity

Who are you? If you don't know,
how can anyone else?

A Brief Exchange

Approaching me with something
on his mind, a friend says, "I don't
think that I can ever change."

"Do you want to?"

"No."

"Well, there you have it." The
    prayer answered.

Replica Masses

The world of pacing. One mass,
roller bags and smartphones attached,
one to each appendage, going in one direction.
    A near-exact replica
moving in the opposite direction.

One man with two metal legs bounces along
ably in the migration. A testament to his
will and the imagination that sought to make
whole what some more destructive force
had torn asunder. One can only speculate
that it was his own government—odds being
    what they are these days.

The woman with her cleaning cart comes
down the concourse ready to tidy the
    untidiness of others.
    She appears almost invisible.
Stealth duty, as most lives of such work.

Some move along half-asleep. Others, young and in
love, cling to each other and smile in delight.
One baby screams loudly, pronouncing her
    disdain for airports and car seats.

There are the young, with their perceived
invincible backs carrying gigantic packs
strapped to their bodies as they wend their
way through the crowd—any sudden turn
disrupting the flow as their humpbacks disrupt
some poor passing stranger's equilibrium.

My favorite sights are the disembarking

passengers as they come out of the jetway.
Equilibrium in question, they stagger a bit,
gaze in both directions, trying to discern
which mass they should join next.

It's hard to tell if anyone is moving in the
    right direction,
    for the right purpose.
But there is no doubt that we are on the move.
Where it all will stop, only that crying infant
may live long enough to know. What will
she say we accomplished with all this
    daily coming and going?
Not much, is my guess.

For all the marketing of beauty products
and fashion, the masses are humdrum
and shabby, more often than not. The wise
Carpenter—right again. No one arrayed with
the simple beauty of the lilies of the field.
    My own simple beauty,
    coated over in platinum SkyMiles.

Movings

Merton never could quite sort out the
monk's life. Is it really the work of
Christ, or the comfort and security of
the cloister, that keeps the monk in his
solitary place? All my movings beg the same
question. Am I doing the work or trying
to find comfort where there is none? Seeking
    simplicity by complicating life.
Where must I be to begin again
    to be?

Is It I?

A world economy is devastating land
and sea and all its creatures.
What drives this ruination?
    Is it I?
My country is obsessed with its greatness
as a nation while crumbling at the seams.
Who owns this blind ambition?
    Is it I?
Religion condemns far more than it redeems
and wallows in its shallow piety and prayers.
Who follows these visionless guides?
    Is it I?
Homes are cluttered, ugly, and see no hope
of care, not unlike their blood-entwined inhabitants.
What breeds this slothful carelessness?
    Is it I?
My mirror reflects a hollow shell of
greed and pride, prejudice and indifference.
Who is to change this lot of mine?
    It is I.

Libera Shuffle

Five hours late, the afternoon flight
    becomes the night flight.
I select shuffle for the playlist "inflight."
As the last red horizon fades in the west,
out my window to the east are
distant, pink-illuminated clouds
as some mighty thunderhead asserts
    its presence in the night.

Lead kindly light, lead on.
So long thou power has led me.
    Lead thou me home.

Smoothly sailing the distant storm
seems a kindly light—a welcome, lovely companion
for the ride home. A free show
for those with enough presence to see
as dualistic ions in their positive and negative pull
debate whether to shake us from our comfort.

(A remarkable commentary on nature's dualism
versus the pathetic, ubiquitous dualism of political
posturing.)

    From the flight deck—rough air.
Word and deed—the seatbelt light illuminates.
The ions hear the boys' crescendo, the end all,
begging divine mercy for the darkness of life.

Miserere, recordare Misere nobis
    Confutatis, maledictis
    Confutatis, maledictis!

    ...Not tonight.

Suddenly, the lightning disappears.
The dark, calm night presides after all.
The seatbelt light off again, then on again, as
we make our way from above the clouds
    back to *terra firma*. The traveler lands
safely, picks up his bit of baggage, drives silently
toward Mount a-Dora-ble, and finds his way
    through the dark house
to his own bed, crowded with dogs who confirm
    their delight at his return.
He hears, still playing in his mind, the gentle pleas,
    and gives thanks.

Salva me. Lead thou me on.

Checklist Traveler

The itinerary-driven traveler, checking off the site
from the list, seems the point of their venturing from
someplace that perhaps is not fully home.
It is not clear if the beauty of a place is appreciated
    or even observed.
It is clear the contemplation that might have been
    was lost for the next thing on the list.
    They scurry along.
No time to waste. Sites remain to be checked off.
Oblivious to the relaxed culture around them as
they push their way ever onward.

Final Heartbeat

Drug-free yet oddly feeling
lost. Psychedelic moodiness.
 One seven-billionth
of the ever-consuming
depletion of all. Where
is the simplicity of grace?
When no one's life will
be even more lost than it is with me,
 let me pass into the earth.

Not depressed. Not suicidal exactly.
Inexplicable melancholy
for the inexplicable contradictions
of absolute joy and overwhelming
evil. My mood will pass quickly
enough. No history suggests
 the evil ever will.
Yet, it is the destiny of joy
and the heart of the prophet
to bequeath a faithful, grateful
heart. May the final heartbeat and
brainwave still hold to sober joy,
 uncommercialized,
  given freely.

Focus

Focus, man! You are making no progress
in the human experience, juggling as you do
your laptop, iPad, smartphone—
all working to make us dumber, less
engaged, but connected to consumerism's
    "land of more."

Whatever is going on with all the screens that your
eyes and finger dart from, one to the other, to
manage, all you are really managing is
diminished capacity. Focus, man!

Cussin' Work

It is painful—watching workers work
    when they don't know how to work.
They abuse their young, strong bodies
by making work out of work
    that could be avoided
    with a little more brain than brawn.
The end result of their labors—mediocrity,
    always behind schedule and
    cussin' everything that
is reflected in their anger-filled gaze.
They don't need to learn to do it better. After all,
    it's just a job to tide them over
    until they win the lottery.

Pseudonym's Story

Hi. I'm August. From childhood, I have been faithful
to a Church that hasn't been particularly faithful
    to me or to my decades-long partner.
We met in Church and have been blessed to live
our life in communities that loved us,
embraced us, and hoped that I could serve them
as a faithful pastor. The Church would have none of it—
    neither of blessing our life together
nor of pondering the notion that the Spirit
    may even call the likes of us.

Inherently, we knew that God's grace was sufficient and
that we should never enter into a marriage
where we questioned our very nature. Instead,
    we chose the life
    of fidelity together.
We remain puzzled by the obsession with our kind—
perhaps hopeful that the Church will one day see
how selectively and narrowly scripture has been used to
    condemn us.
We remain more than a little fearful that children have to face
the same fears as countless others before them,
    who knew that to be different
was to be alien from those they loved and
was even to brutalized by them and others.
We offer peace from our home to yours,
that your children may know
what the Church seems yet unwilling to bestow—
    the unconditional love of Christ.

USA Today

The world section paints a bleak picture —
    ISIL killing and being killed.
    Ebola frightening the frightful.
The money section has a different headline:
    "Consumer confidence surprisingly strong."
Military might working its magic.

Uber Austin

"Ever been to Austin?" the Uber driver asked.
My companions quickly said no. I never got
the chance to say, "Too many times." He was
    off and running.
A nonstop discourse on all that made Austin
something that, by his reckoning, was different
    than the rest of Texas.
Looks pretty much the same as other Texas cities to me —
though not confined to Texas by any means.
    Overbuilt and overpriced.
    Smog and traffic and
    pretense to mask the cookie-cutter lifestyle.
The underclass lurking in ubiquitous despair.

Blanco, TX and Lake Diane MI, 2016–2019

Party of the RPC and the 2016 Election Cycle
(A reflection on warmongering "pro-lifers" and the procession of those who find it ever harder to identify with party or religious institution)

Am I really so radical?
I want the neocon out of my bedroom;
Wall Street out of my local bank;
Walmart out of my sight altogether;
    the county clerk
to sign my government-issued marriage license;
the pro-lifer to include the innocents of Syria and
    to take every murderer off death row.

(Abortion is a sadness, but let it be between the doctor, the woman, and those she loves to cope. No one needs the immoral government pretending to know moral absolutes.)

Am I really so radical?
I want to conserve the beauty of the Earth
    and all its creatures;
neighbor to care for neighbor
    without constructing walls;
soldiers to stand at ease
instead of being sent off
in soul-surrendering missions
    for the war profiteers.

(War is a sadness that exemplifies pride's refusal to listen and honor dignity; a never-ending, diabolical quid pro quo of greedy trade deals, weapon deals, power deals.)

Am I really so radical?

I want an economy that sustains
    rather than drains;
a farm where the soil grows,
not degrading the already degraded
    muddy polluted rivers;
a religion that *is* love—
    simply that;
a faith that knows that we don't know what we don't know;
an inherent humility where
    less is enough.

I guess I am too radical.
I don't get any time on cable news.
No super-Pac would have me,
    nor I them.
I don't give a damn about building
a presidential library to honor my greatness.
I don't need anyone to fear me.

I am a party member of radical progressive conservatives—
    rad-pro-cons.
I am for the ninety-nine percent—
most of whom seem to have deleted me
from their contacts on their
    not-so-smart phone.

You will have to drop by.
    I'm not on Facebook
and I don't fit with Twitter.
    You'll find me sitting
in the sunshine. Living peaceably.
    Loving life—as best I can.
    Loving you.

Faulty Foundations

We bow to the great philanthropists
    and their foundations.
Grant money, proud sponsorships,
association with the champagne reception crowd
    —we lap it up. To borrow a line from
cowboy poet JB Allen (RIP), "They hold the dole
we can't afford to lose."

There belies a faulty foundation for those
large and small—their fiduciary agents ensuring
maximum return of billions on trillions of
invested capital while handing out
photo-op-sized checks
    of the returns to
    make their image shine.

The books are carefully guarded,
    though on occasion,
we get a glimpse of where that money breeds:
    prisons for profit,
    payday loan sharks, derivatives,
subsistence farmers driven from their land,
    weapons, dirty energy,
retail giants in all their exploitation.
Thus perpetuating with their capital
the poverty and ignorance that the myth of purpose
is supposed to help us overcome.

Keep your tainted gains
    where your money is
    —well, you know the rest.

    And by the way—
clergy, wake up! Your pension funds

    blindly funding on Monday
the evils preached against
        on Sunday.

New Day

There never was a good old day
though I've heard tell of such days
    all my years,
Of some romantic epoch when
    there was peace;
all were employed in great jobs they loved;
schools were filled with (by my memory,
plenty of ornery but) unarmed,
    hopeful leaders and
    dutiful citizens of tomorrow;
churches were filled with the faithful.

In those good old days, there
    were a lot of blind old days.
Blind to the destruction of serial warfare.
Blind to the exploitation of workers
    whose desperation left bereft their
    yearning for dignity.
Blind to how rapidly and carelessly we
    drew down the bounty of our planetary home.
Blind to how much racism and bigotry
    sat piously in exclusionary pews.

There is always good and bad in every day.
Whether the net is worse now is mighty hard to say.

(It doesn't look too good at the moment).

Romanticizing the past helps no one.
Disdain for the present concedes defeat—
    a dereliction of what is ours to do.

Whatever the day—be it
edging ever so meekly toward good or

careening recklessly toward the bad—
we have our seminal duty.
    Bear witness to pain.
    Care for the least.
Live in gratitude, not for your share of
    market goods,
but for the beauty and generosity that
surrounds you and sustains you.
Live in hope of finding within
    the Spirit of peace,
and once found, live peaceably.

Such is the work; such is the gift
that must be renewed at dawn
    and left in trust at day's end
    for the dawn to come.

The Thriller

The antonym of thrill is bore.
Semantics is not a pure science.
As movies go, I am a frequent admirer,
though I am bewildered by the thriller
and refuse to rent anything with a
    gun, tank, or fireball
    on the cover.

Perhaps if we stopped being
entertained by violence,
we might make less of it.
    Risk a little boredom;
    save the world.

Party Animals

    I admit it,
a drink helps at these occasions.
    Crowds are not my thing.
I attempt to be sociable while the
useless talk gets ever louder and either
    giddier or
    stepping into belligerence.
Some can't resist talking about their
    favored or despised politician.
No insight. Just babble.

When escape seems possible,
I re-enter creation, void of the noise.
    The thought comes—
"He passes by the wordless, silent landscape and hears
the most profound call that can be."
Is that my line, or did I hear it sometime—somewhere?
    No idea. Anyway, it leads to
    peace without the cocktail, and
love for the distance between me and the party animals.

Rabid Passion

We've all known them.
Some are our friends—some family.
They latch onto what seems
    impossible and
    don't let go.
They defend the worst of the worst
for the sake of party or religion or ego.
We can know them. We can love them.
    We need not be them.

Care

Can't bottle it, exploit it, or profit from it.
No wonder it's so hard to find.

Mercy

We've tailored godly images to be hateful
and then prayed for godly blessings for our wars.
"Good God!" isn't a curse.
    It's the soul's cry.
    It's the mercy we deny.

On a Line by Raimond Gaita
(A reflection on the Primo Levi account of Charles and *Lakmaker*,
days before the liberation of Auschwitz, from *A Common Humanity*
and a quote from a lecture by Gaita at the 2015 Melbourne Writer's
Festival)

The peacemakers may be blessed,
but they are dismissed out of hand
by press, pundit, politician, and public,
    all too easily
    all too frequently.
Dismissed as naïve are such notions as
    common humanity
    for a common good,
which offers uncompromised compassion.
But the great acts of compassion are
exemplified in the worst of suffering—
not some pie-in-the-sky utopia.
    "We are not in hippy-land. We are in Auschwitz."

Charles, with nothing to gain but holding
fast to his human dignity, ensures
the dignity of the wretchedly ill
Lakmaker as he gently cares for him
    "with the tenderness of a mother."
    "We are not in hippy-land. We are in Auschwitz."

Remind the skeptic that there are indeed
    two ways.
When pressed by evil—hate, with all its forms
    of violence and condescension.
When pressed by evil—love, and hold fast to
    your own humanity and redeem it in others.
    "We are not in hippy-land. We are in Auschwitz."

Moving to the Edge
(For Aurie Mitchell West)

        i.

My friend Aurie asked, "Have I fallen off the cliff?"
She was once so sure of dogma and doctrine,
    a pharisee—self-proclaimed.
She wobbled upon moving up to the edge,
where the next step led—
where that last step always leads—
    falling into grace perfected.
Her beloved dogma and doctrine
seen for what they were to her—
    shackles,
    shattered to pieces by the fall.
The soul set free to be.

        ii.

Age has its advantages,
though many a man and many a woman
squander what it has to offer,
    too locked into pride-image-ego
to see the gift within. As Ruby Sales says,
"Hindsight, insight foresight"
    all gifts of age,
    turning "I sight" into "we sight."
Living the length, the width, the depth.
The soul set free to be.

        iii.

What an odd mix that looks to you
    with affection.
Heretic and heathen.
Left-wing, right-wing, wing-clipped.
Those with everything, it would seem.

Those with nothing, it would seem.
Gay, straight, and the not quite sure.
Felons and the squeaky clean,
    or so we think.
You move beyond Church walls,
beyond the confines of your family home
to wander amid the west Texas landscape
    of odd characters—
    those newly arrived and
    those rooted for generations.
To those of us who see what's there,
    you share with us
    that gift too rare.
The soul set free to be.

No Denial

    Not even five o'clock.
The loud man at the bar
dominates the room. Too friendly
with the bartender. Mostly, she politely
ignores him—going about her business.
She, it seems to me,
should have cut him off by now.
Instead, she offers him another.
    Finally, he stumbles to go.
His departure long, drawn out,
    and boisterous.
The damage over sixty bucks.
As helpless strangers to his ills,
we see him totter up the stairs,
    just as loud,
as he approaches the more-sober world.
We are quietly stuffing ourselves;
    glad to see him go.
"Would you like to see our dessert menu?"
    "We'll pass" (this time).
We leave a while later.
    An undramatic, quiet departure.
    Carrying similar tonnage up the stairs.
A drunkard and two gastronomic gluttons.
More in common than we can deny.

Baggage-Burden

I can't travel anywhere without
    being bewildered by
the self-inflicted baggage-burden
hauled by what seems more than most.

If we are hauling that much onto
    the crowded plane
when we travel not even a fortnight,
what are we hauling around in
    our crowded minds?

Where your baggage is,
    there will be your burden also.
Pack light. It's a long journey, and it's amazing
    how little we really need
    to find joy along the way.

Francis in Washington

They politely applaud. His presence
    brings them to their feet. As you watch,
you know they will do nothing with his words.
    (Well, they will dismiss them.)
They will shake his hands,
    happy for any photo-op with
        someone so important on the global stage.

Months pass. The election cycle
    spins into high gear.
The promises are nauseating.
The rhetoric, hideous.
Press and pundits a bit too giddy
from all the fodder pitched their way.
    And sure enough,
America remains hell-bent, defining
us in our superior right of might.

    Pressing ever onward and
bearing witness for the forgotten,
Francis washes and kisses the feet of
    prisoner and poor,
    Muslim and Hindu.
Riding off in his little Fiat for another day
    of pleading for our soul.

While he naïvely
    (or so we tell ourselves)
looks for paths of peace,
we press on in fury-frenzy
in our never-ending quest,
asserting, for all the world to see,
    supreme arrogance,
        trillions spent and sold on warring madness,

    condescension for the mere idea of peace.

Jesus said, "Forgive them—they know not
    what they do."
We know exactly what we do, and yet
pompously, we pray for God to bless America.

Oh, Francis, may we "be one in loving and forgiving,
with hopes and dreams as true and high as thine,"
    seeking, finally, the path of peace
      for their land and for mine.

Raspberries from My Garden

Oh, how I love you,
    but what patience you require!
    Months pass until
you bear large clusters of your tiny fruit.
Yet, in some master plan with sunlight,
only a few red fruits are ripe for the picking
    on any given day.
    You require my daily attention.
Skip even a day, and you rot and drop
your fruit for the creatures of the ground
    that happen by.
Your prickly stems force my care.
I hear your vines telling me,
    "Look how tending well is rewarded."
I should have known, something as
wonderful as you would know
    that sacred call of
    creation's dawn.

Boiling Pot

It brings me a certain unmatched joy
to watch something as simple as
the Cajun-rooted partner of mine
eating crab. Undaunted by spines and
hard shells with their nooks and crannies, he
    cracks and digs and picks
    every little morsel.
Nothing wasted that can be digested.
All the while, his face reflecting a contentment
that is little different from the dogs given a
    nice, meaty bone.
    No rush to finish.
More patience than he has for almost anything else.

Enjoy the feast, my friend. Neither you nor I
nor the planet can afford such indulgence
    without some deliberate
    self-imposed infrequency.

"Your blindness doesn't seem to impact your
ability to pick crab," I say.

Your hands continue their work.
"Don't need to see to eat crab."

When the last bit is gone, there is only the
clean-up, as the final blessing is invoked.
    "Ç'est bon!"

On Lines by Khalifa Al-Khadr
(A reflection on Khalifa Al-Khadr, a student at Allepo University during the 2011 Syrian uprising, from an article by Murtaza Hussain, posted on *The Intercept*, 23 October 2016.)

The young students wanted a freedom they didn't have.
    Ideology was not their cause.

"The reason we rose up was to just kill fear. To kill
this fear that we had all been living under as a society."

Fear ensures its fateful end,
    giving us what we feared.
The tyrants of power meet such fears with force,
which leads to greater fears and greater failures.
It seems that tyrannical powers would rather see all
go up in flames around them than to concede
to a humility that honors dignity above all else.
Assad may be one of the tyrannical puppets
    now on stage,
but he is hardly alone. American democracy strains
under the fear-machinery of war, under the
    oligarch's oppressive control. Perhaps,
most horrifying of all, our wallowing in complicity—
    ensuring our balanced stock portfolio's returns.

I pledge allegiance to the mutual fund and
to the security for which it stands.

As Walter Bruggemann postulates, "Market ideology
wants us to go to NFL games and never think."
    But I digress.

We cannot kill fear and no "ism" can make peace last.
Can't we, like nature, just blow it away and start over?
    No, as nature heals itself,

fear and war and tyranny do not.
    (A lesson we should have learned by now.)

Peace comes only by each person planting seeds of
    peace and tending to them well.
Cherishing the other's life as equal to our own.
    (Seen and unseen.)
It may cost us everything. We can never retire
from an investment made in a moment
of optimistic idealism. It cannot be bought or sold.

And yet these simple facts remain:
    Without it, we are not free.
    With it, each is free to be.
Stop marching. Start planting.

General Nonsense

Sometimes I can't believe my ears. The TV
wasn't on for two minutes this Sunday morning
when I heard a well-known preacher say,
"You are a warrior facing battle. Pray to the general
every morning for strength for the battle."

Holy shit!

(The subject of such an exclamation does, in fact, offer more
holy food to Mother Earth than what these poor sheep are
being fed.)

His Sermon on the Mount clearly reads differently
from mine. I don't recall,
    "Blessed are the prayer warriors,
    for they shall march over [insert your
    most despised group here]."

Even blessed Paul's analogy of
armor was hardly an endorsement for "God,
    our General, who art in the war room."

I recall some rather noble fruits of the Spirit,
and I think it is time for Christians to
fertilize well around their roots
and start producing something good
and sweet and worthy of their namesake.

    More holy shit. Fewer warriors.

Charity

How can we thrive and not just survive?
Keep it alive as sweet as the hive,
love for a brother against our druthers
and for the other who wants to smother.

We cling to hate when it seems too late
to find in our state the more noble fate
of loving, like Zen, the colors of men,
the beautiful wren, the fox in the den.

Shedding our skin for where we have been,
may dignity win, despite all the spin
of boisterous news of particular views,
lighting the fuse of empire's ruse.

Calling our bluff that we all are so tough,
we take pride in the stuff that flies off the cuff,
hurting our chances for kindlier glances
in rhythmical dances without all the lances.

But just so we know where we should go,
we leaven the dough with seeds that we sow
in absolute clarity, our humble, pure charity
found in such rarity, this high calling, verity.

More Evil Dreams of Night

I wish I could just dream of
    beautiful meadows,
    crystal clear streams,
bountiful harvests with food for all.
These are the dreams of my days.

Be it the evils of our time, as seen
in every news source, or
my own evils lurking within,
    it remains fact—
My dreams in the dark of night too often
    are sinister and
violent. Good never triumphs
in these dreams, any more than
it seems to with every clash
of hubris perpetuated on the
    world stage.
No matter what, the evil forces
in my dreams cannot be killed.
They are crushed or shot, only to rise
    again and pursue me.

I awaken. Not so much to fright, but
certainly to some frustration
that these vivid, evil images
    persist in my mind.
And I am repeatedly persuaded, in my
awakening:
    You cannot kill
    your way to peace.
This must be the meaning
    of the dream.

When will we stop buying the lie

    that we can?
When will we risk our own
    401K, our mutual fund,
to be sure that we do not fund
what we purport to abhor?
    We are complicit.
The dreams only validate
    the reality.

Can we believe that
    abortion is murder
and war is not? Yet
the politicians of
    pro-life make war.
And, one must observe,
the politicians of
    pro-choice make war too.

Too many jobs depend
on a war machine to destroy
    anyone, anything, anywhere.
Too many jobs depend
on growing an economy
    of mass consumption—
in itself a war against the planet
    that sustains us.
And so, we war and we consume.
Where it will end, I do not know.
If I can't dream of
    beautiful meadows,
    crystal clear streams,
bountiful harvests with food for all,
    this much is sure:
I must work for those things
    while I am awake.

Media Storm

    i. Reality Television
Take the talentless.
Emotionally charge them.
Feed them to the mindless.
    Repeat.

    ii. Tabloid Journalism
Betray journalistic integrity.
Peddle in groupthink fear agendas.
Feed them to the mindless.
    Repeat.

    iii. Talk Radio
Frame issues through blinders.
Scapegoat the "other."
Feed it to the mindless.
    Repeat.

    iv. Christian Broadcasting
Preach your own blessed state.
Judge the "unworthy."
Feed it to the mindless.
    Repeat.

    v. 2016 Post-election
Avoid soul-searching.
Blame Putin.
Feed it to the mindless.
    Repeat.

The Demagogue

My kingdom come.
    Thy kingdom go.
On Earth as it is in hell.

The Refugee

I do not belong to any one time
    or to any one culture.
I am with you always. For every inch
gained in one place in one time,
    for my basic dignity,
an inch or more is conceded in
another place and time.
While it seems that this need not be so,
    it remains the truth
of my life, my suffering, my fate.

    Atheist and idolatrous regimes,
religious pretense, market forces,
retribution and retaliation, all conspire
    to take the little bit I have
and steal or destroy it and my meager means
of survival, setting me on a path of
despair. I am sometimes complicit with
these forces. I bought their lie that
violence could improve my lot. That
revolution would bring me peace. That
the trade deal would bring prosperity.
    I am more often
an unwitting victim. My age, my already
tattered body, are given no consideration.
If I am starved, maimed, or killed, it
    matters not.

In all likelihood, I'll not be counted.
At best, just some general statistic
to be estimated, according to whichever
side of history is keeping tabs.
    I am hopeless and lost.

If you don't want me wandering
    across your border, swimming to
your shore, then think carefully about
what you do when you consign your
proxy to the greedy, the prideful,
    the moneyed interests
who can only conceive of more.
    Who affirm their absolute authority.
Who are willing to exploit anyone and
anything, anywhere, and at any cost.
Their guns and bombs encircle me.
Their drones persist to remind me that
    I am at their mercy—
though they have no mercy.
They are not content to leave me in
my simple existence. My poverty is
no shield to those who must wield
    their reckless control.

I don't want to be your tired and poor.
    I don't want to be another
huddled mass upon your teaming shore.
    I simply want to live my life here,
devoid of the destruction brought on by
illusory moral pretense of the narcissistic,
megalomaniacs in their tit-for-tat games.
    Forgive me
when my own actions have made me
    complicit in such evil.

May I have the humility to love and forgive
as I leave the flaming rubble,
    the stolen plot of land,
for a journey whose end is unsure.
I cannot know now, whether I will find
    arms of welcome or
    more rejection and death.
It will likely be the latter. Still, I
must set out, fearful and with little hope,
    for it is the only choice
given to me, your refugee.

Tick-tock

    If time were money,
then we would have no poor.
The poor have time enough.
    They punch in, punch out.
Time clocks feed the
databank that prints a
paltry compensation for
    their time.

The rich would have us believe
that time is money. The clock
always ticking. Awaiting a
    greater accumulation
at the end of the each and
every day. It is not the day clock
they hear ticking. It is the
    time-bomb of greed
ticking-ticking-ticking.
    Waiting to explode.

Mercy's Accounting

When you think about it, the Church's
notion of forgiveness is really very often
    a credit/debit transaction.
We like legislative minimal sentences
in the Church, as well as in the state.
It may be so many "Hail Mary's" or
"Our Fathers." Yes, protestants, too,
are guilty of this, as you preach
    guilt and condemnation
    by category.
And it is often the most "evangelically
supported" politician who exacts the
harshest penalties for "repeat offenders,"
    as a directive from the constituency.

In case we haven't noticed, both the sacrificial
lamb and scapegoating were cast out by
    the carpenter of Galilee.
"Which is easier to say, 'Get up and walk'
    or 'Your sins are forgiven'?"

Jesus doesn't explore people's guilt and
delve into the detail of sin.
    They seek mercy.
    Mercy is granted them.
Mercy is shown even before it's requested.
If he, who knows the heart, does this,
what does it say about us,
    we who do not know?
Forgive, and then forgive, and then
    forgive some more.
That was the instruction.
    No double-entry accounting
was ever part of the transaction.

Thoughts on a New Economy

      i. Lessons Not Learned
War. Stupidity that just keeps on giving:
    birth defects; cancer;
    nerve damage;
tearing limbs off; implanting
shrapnel; making toxic—land and water;
    chemicals; radiation; land mines;
    cluster bombs; fire pits;
destroying vital infrastructure—
    hospitals, water and sewage treatment.
The ultimate folly of technology
that assails generation
    after generation.
And what have we learned since
the world wars and Vietnam?
    Nothing.
Peace remains a joke—a mere byword
of the politician and party.
Security an illusion—a calculated lie
of the politician and party.
    War the ever-constant reality
for us and for undeserving victims—
    children and
the children yet unborn.

      ii. Lessons Learned
    Consume less. If you have
to have a list to keep your tasks
organized, consider reprioritizing
    what chews away at your time.
Support the farmer whose animals
are well cared for, whose land and
    water are well cared for.
    Garden if you can. Plant

a little bit of this and a little bit of that.
Do it with children whenever possible.
If you have an organic garden, share
    your skills with others.
Avoid making Monsanto and the like happy.
    Better a few weeds than no bees.
What does your local community need?
    Work to make it happen.
How complicit is your local
economy to the war machine?
    If it is complicit, work to turn
swords into plowshares. Factories
can turn out things besides
    armaments.
Foster apprenticeships for the
basic skills needed for the community.
Not everyone needs a college education.
    Build well and maintain. End the
bulldozer-mindset. Have your church/club
buy a blighted house and remake it a
home for someone in the community.
Life can go on without a growing GDP.
    Stop pretending it cannot.
Forget Wells Fargo, Citibank, Chase.
    Forget mutual funds.
Sacrifice a few points of return for
a distancing of the great greed machine.
Keep your money local. Press to start
    local, public banks.
Don't depend on the great foundations
to solve local problems or address
international calamities fixed to their agenda.
    Know where the principal
is invested before accepting a dime
from any grant or foundation.
    Refuse tainted gains.

If you see trash in the parking lot,
    pick it up. Don't wait for the
wind to blow it out of your sight.
    It is yours to do.
Stop defending the party. Don't
let the PACs influence your vote.
Dare to have conversations about
politics and religion without having
    to persuade anyone.
    If you believe in war,
read and listen to Wendell Berry,
study Dorothy Day, Thomas Merton,
    MLK.
If you can't wrap your head around
the Bible and the economy,
    read and listen to
Walter Brueggemann and Ellen Davis.
    If you think you possess
the whole truth, awaken! You don't.
Be kind. Practice empathy.
    Cook for those you love and
for those you are called to love.
    Connect. Share a simple meal.
Keep a tidy house and kitchen.
Wash dishes by hand. Stop supporting
the disposable goods industry.
    Sponsor a child's music, art, and dance
lessons. Attend their recitals.
Sing. Clash a cymbal. Beat a drum.
Do it joyfully. Write something to offer
encouragement. Give your gifts freely.
    Ponder the created world.
It has much to teach us about our
    disconnected reality from it.
Keep religious life honest. Don't
check your mind at door and don't

club others over the head with your
    limited, narrow viewpoint.
We all see through the glass darkly.
    Support charities that stand
unequivocally for nonviolence and
uncompromised dignity for all.
    As Mr. Berry suggests,
ask questions with no convenient
and readily available answers.
In this, you will discover some
    of your own ignorance and
some needed patience to think about
the mainstream marketing of answers.
Abandon the predestined fates
    of optimism and pessimism.
Live in hope. Have faith in mysteries
beyond your ability to comprehend.
    Weep for your own complicity.
And when the last tear has dried,
    act with care. Repeat as needed.
Contemplate what you can do and do it.
    When you stumble, try again.
End the day in gratitude for what is,
    peaceably, in your own heart.
Greet the new day with what can be,
    and in gratitude, begin again.

    iii. Care-fully
As Wendell Berry says,
"Care cannot be an industrial product
    or an industrial output."
Nor can it be wrapped up in a
cause. Fighting for a cause may
bring its warriors pride, but it
will never bring care to the fore.
    Care requires four things:

love, patience, awareness of our ignorance,
    and action informed by
    the first three.
Such care makes peace
and the wellbeing of our planetary home possible.
    Make peace possible.

Off the Pavement

    All roads lead to empire.
The way is paved, though it's not without
its potholes. It is interconnected
with the industrial economy.
It has its share of blight and boredom.
    If you feel road rage, you will
know you are on the empire highway.
It is supposed to serve efficiency over
beauty, though even efficiency is often
    compromised for the lowest bid.

The indigenous foot trails, overgrown
mostly these days, can be spotted
along these highways, but it takes a
    keen eye and willing heart
to see them. It takes resolve to set
out on them, to see where they will
lead. They lead to creation's
juxtaposition of simplicity and majesty.
    They bear witness to care.

Easter 2017

    Ah, glorious Son-rise!
Your Easter day reminds us that
the forgiveness offered on Friday
was not recanted then on Sunday.
    You did not get even.
You did not command a proportional response—
some divine retribution for the bad treatment you'd received.
You did not incite hate or fear.
    Instead, by some accounts,
you tidied up the garden,
walked with friends along their journey,
broke bread together—still blessing the free gifts of creation.
    To us, the deniers, doubters, and confused,
you speak our name and offer us these resurrection words:
    Peace be with you.

Thoughts on a June Morning

    Die with gratitude
for the gift given of life
among the beauty and grace
of the free gifts of creation.
    Your place is here.
Let each breath, to the last,
enliven a heart of gratitude.
Give yourself back to
Mother Earth, who
    bore you,
    nurtured you,
and will do her best, against
the odds of our careless ways,
    to cast her seeds of life
and bloom a million
or a billion seasons more.

Holding Hands with Amos
(Honoring prophetic voices past and present)

    We are not casual observers.
We have existed from the beginning.
Our attention is drawn into the
complexities of life. There is little
that we fear and much that we ponder.

We are an inconvenient truth
that upsets and challenges
    the narrative of exploitation
and careless devotion.
We are the proverbial thorn
in neat and tidy orthodoxies.
We seek mightily to hear the voices
that speak another word from the
lies of purchased power, the hubris of
establishment groupthink, the evil
    of warring madness.
We seek never to give our
precious time and meager treasure
    to the machine of greed,
grinding its cruel wheel 24-7-365.

We know too well that most ears are stopped
and eyes blinded to anything that
    challenges the status quo,
even when the world is burning down around us.
    We lament this greatly,
yet it does not deter our work.

Few in history have challenged
    the powerful like we have,
        the poets of peace and justice.

We are the stream of refreshing waters
flowing clear and strong to an uncertain end.
We are the wind that comes and goes in the gentle
refreshment of hope and the stormy gale of action.
We are the fire that refines and consumes
the mountainous ores of deceit.
Against the religious rallying cry
    for yet another "just war,"
we seek paths to peace in the solitary heart.
While power uses disparate voices
    to sow chaos and fear,
we refuse to scapegoat. Our tent is
open to the misfits, the poor, and the oppressed,
those seeking to live peaceably
    with all creation.
We celebrate color, quirks, and eccentricities.
We know that love can bridge
    what no wall can confine.

We come in every shade, faith, and gender.
We wander the streets of Calcutta and the
deserts of Iraq. We knock at the doors of
Beijing, Moscow, and Washington.
Our voices rise up in song from
    within the prison walls.
We stop for the beaten on the Jericho road.
    We weep for the refugee, and yes,
consider the sparrow that falls from its nest.

It is the norm for the powerful
    to seek to ignore us.
When they cannot, we are ridiculed,
our words distorted, our vision mocked.
    Yet we are undeterred.
If one of us is silenced,
another is moved to carry on.

Our great reward is the kindness of a
 helping hand.
Our hand is outstretched.
It is always outstretched and welcoming.
 Will you reach out and clasp it?

Draft Horse Journal

Across the neighbor's field,
we mostly ignore what is going on.
There is a mighty green machine
with an engine of over 400 horsepower,
    roaring,
foraging its way through the soybean field,
with dust spewing forth from the beast
at such a density, one could suffocate
if caught in its wake.
    Horsepower by fire and exhaust.

The farmer has but one use for the beans.
Great long trucks (also of fire and exhaust)
transport the bounty to the grain elevator,
where it will turn the bean into green.
This is the cash crop. The farmer won't
be selling this on a roadside stand or
putting it on his table.

This is just a matter-of-fact telling.
    It is of no interest to us.
We do not praise it or condemn it.

Our day starts early. The older boys
finish their chores quickly and come
to dress us for the day's work.
There are eight of us. We work in pairs.
    They know us all by name.
With our collars and work harnesses on,
we are hitched up to the wagons.
We head to the field full of bright pumpkins.

In the field, there are eight or so of them as well.
They, too, work as a team. Even the

four-year-old girl wanders with the others
and picks the small fruit when she sees
one she can handle. The old dog, Amos,
who wandered along, finds a high spot in the field
and keeps a watchful eye whenever he can
manage to stay awake. They all look
content to us, just as we are content.

The children giggle when the dad,
farting loudly, hollers in the old Swiss dialect,
    "Thunder in the west!"
    He smiles at their amusement.
All continue their work.

We stand patiently in the field, moving
slowly along with them. They begin filling
the first wagon, and then they call the teams
to move along with their work as
each of the wagons is filled.
Eight horses, men, women, and
children power. These Amish
keep us and tend us, and we are a
vital part of their economy. The bright,
orange crop is sold at their roadside,
cooked into breads, cakes, and pies.
And it's the big cash crop going to
grocery stores in the towns and cities.

    For our part,
we kick up but little dust, and we
fertilize as we clomp along. When
the wagons are full, we pull the
load back to the homestead, get
a deep drink from the trough. The same
boys who dressed us remove the tack as
we stand ready for the feed that we helped

put in the ground some months before and
that solar power and humus made bountiful.

This is just a matter-of-fact telling.
    It is of no interest to most.
We praise it for the circle of life that it is.

Elegy to Bob Huffaker (1936–2018)

There are some we meet—some even kin—for whom
we ask, how am I ever going to love this person?
    Love being the great calling of us all.

Then there is the person that comes into our lives whose
heart comes pouring out of mischievous eyes
    and a griping bear-hug embrace.
Love comes easily then, as our love came to you.

A heart, weak by nature, yet intense and passionate in life.
Generous to imperfect friends and children.
Bold enough to call bullshit bullshit, without any hesitation—
    such judgements reserved for the pretentious.

Pretentious you were not. Lovely you were.
And while that body could finally not go on another moment,
    that sweet embrace that was you is still, and shall remain,
holding us tightly for what remains of our journey.

Peace to your gentle heart.

Betrayal

It takes so little. The bickering begins.
For those who yearn for and
    hope for peace,
it can seem hopeless when those
closest to us cause us to want to
    retreat into seclusion.
To resign from the human race.
To escape unkind and thoughtless
words spewed in cutting contempt.

We wish it were just the ego getting
in the way of a greater humility,
but the fact remains that, rationality
abandoned, the inexplicable
    urge to be cruel erupts
in total disproportion to the moment.
Even the ego recognizes the ridiculousness
of it all, but steps in to assure that
    no apology is necessary.
We were right to lash out, however
silly the trigger that set all this in motion.

We ignore or forget or forgive. Or we
file it away in the done-me-wrong file
for future reference. Whatever we do with
    these jabs and stabs
of inconsideration, this simple fact remains:
    We have betrayed peace yet again.

Tweet-tweet

My god, I hate Twitter. If you want
to condense words, write some poetic symmetry.
The so called clever-class tweeting
    the drivel-drip, unwired to
reflective thought, being retweeted
in yet more unreflective thought
to the cause-charged masses
    isn't helping.
Surely, you've noticed!

Mr. Lee in Particular

That damned Robert E Lee.
    He's the problem.
How has it taken us this long to see it?
If we can wipe his likeness from the Earth
this country's racist tendencies will be
    gone once and for all.

My anabaptist roots took
    "Make no graven image"
pretty seriously. I could be
persuaded to pass a law that
never allows another memorial
to anyone ever again—be they
on my side of history or against.
For sure, I'm for no more
    presidential libraries to
the greatness of the flawed leaders of war.

    But those anabaptists roots
also instructed me to live

peaceably. I don't want to
destroy our past for the sake
of some imagined future made
    possible by destruction.
Zwingli, Luther, and Knox
all tried that. Didn't work.
(And of course, now we have
statues and monuments to all three.)
Better to learn from history
    than to repeat it ad nauseam.

It is said that Lee believed that the
biggest mistake of his life was
    getting a military education.
Among our many mistakes is to make
his life as hateful and small as our own.

Intervention Obsession

We weep again.
We look in the mirror.
It is hard to have hope,
though I'm sure we must.
Made difficult by those to whom
we've pledged benefit of the doubt,
who then repeat the same old tired lies
that prop up the hubris of exceptionalism
with its heavy toll on the poor and vulnerable,
leaving us more complicit every day with the
evil perpetrated across our beautiful world
and within the cities and villages, where
people are left with no alternative but
to leave home for lands unknown,
for oceans, borders, and walls
that seek to keep them out.
It is hard to have hope.
We look in the mirror.
We weep again.

Sainthood for the Warmonger

    The grand cathedral
hosts the final stage play as another warmonger
is finally embalmed and buried.
Canonized by the faithful as a
    great American—
    a true patriot.
The fountain of praise bubbling over for days.

Here's the problem.

If Jesus loves the little children—
    red and yellow, black and white—
how is it that our great patriots never do?
Their boiling cauldron of destruction
    our gift
to all the little children of the world.

If only they could die out once and
    for all.
How long will our clergy, deans, and bishops
    sanctify the evil?
"Ego te absolvo"—no confession required.

The Time of Old Dogs and the Old Master

The dogs are old now.

(And no, I'm no spring chicken.)

I click and click and click again,
trying to rouse them from their
    now near perpetual laziness.
I continue clicking the leash and
now add loud calling of their names.

Finally, they get up and mosey over to me.
Long gone are the fishtail curves
of their younger days as they raced
    across the concrete floor.
As I hitch them up, they scratch at the door,
    as though I were the hold up.
I remind them that this was my idea.
We wander out. They squat and do
what they assume was theirs to do.
Neighbor dog, Gus, gives a loud bass,
    "Woof-woof."

They ignore him, which only makes
the young Gus give it another try.
They turn around to come back in,
    scratching the door again.
Their unspoken gesture suggests
    I should move a little more quickly.
They seem to have rediscovered
    momentary energy.
Both stand next to the table where
the dog treats reside—looking up at me.
"We did our duty. Let's have the reward."

A few bites, and it's back to napping.
Perhaps they've learned more from me
    than I intended to teach them.
Don starts his *Jane Fonda Walkout*.
Like Gus before, we three ignore him.

   (Penny — RIP May 2004–Dec 2018)
   (Bonnie — RIP May 2004–Jul 2020)

Amish Guard Dogs

The sign outside the Camden bakery reads,
    "Beware of Dog."
This must be to amuse, as the only
dog in sight is lying at the front door
with people stepping around him.
He remains oblivious to the threat of
us outsiders to the Amish life.
    His instinct for danger
has been largely overwritten from years
of living with these peaceable folk.
    No one to teach him mean.

I reach down and pet the ole boy.
    He doesn't move.
Perhaps he's been trained to smell gunpowder
and will spring to action upon the
    slightest whiff.
Yeah, probably not.

Often, I run down the road to pick up
    raspberries and eggs.
No sign about dangerous dogs
at this Amish farm, but
I am surrounded by half a dozen
    red heeler-mix mongrels.
Larger versions of our dog Penny.
Unlike Penny, they seem to love company,
    tails wagging
    so high and fast,
one can imagine their hind ends
coming off the ground. No barking—
    just the same warm greeting
the matron and large brood of children
offer to the patrons coming to "shop local."

You can see in other, less frequent,
less local folks that acute initial fear
of so many approaching dogs, thinking,
"Clearly, I need to beware of dogs."

    Yeah, probably not.
For where your heart is,
    there shall your dogs' be also.

Beech Mountain, NC, December 2019–

The New Year, 2020

    As I cast a shadow,
walking through a small clearing
in the forest, can I ignore
the great shadows of the oaks
and beech and hickory,
whose timeless presence
    form the eternal cycle
of growth, death, and decay?
Underneath their shade
and within their shadows
lives a world of creatures so vulnerable,
    yet so at one with their place.
My paltry, momentary intrusion
    seems so insignificant
when viewed from their world.
Where did the arrogance arise
that gave me disrespecting dominion
over the forest and its creatures,
and by obvious extension,
    all the created world?

Shall I blame a nameless god who
blessed our procreation and
and who asked us, from age to age,
to tend the earth so as to thrive
    and not merely survive?

Surely, dominion does not offer
    unfettered license
    to exploit and rob at will
in our nanosecond of geologic time.

Alas, I am an uneasy being
in the role of dominator,
    so vastly abused
by the adherents of religion and
lords of power who have molded
stewardship into blind neglect
and hyper-exploitation.

Alas, I am an unwilling citizen,
    though too complicit,
for these brokers of destruction in all their forms
who rob souls of their worth
as they feed their ego, extol their pride,
and force their diabolical conformity
    of power and control.

I begin each year in hope
that we shall awaken to a new history.
It begins with little assurance
    of a happy new year,
but it, like all years preceding,
offers joy in simple moments
recognized through the inherent
    beauty that yet survives.
Ah, this beauty is mine to cherish,
    and not mine to destroy.

The Memo

Peter, take a memo.
To: People of Planet Earth
Regarding: Noise Pollution
Earthling Date: 15 Feb 2020

    Stop the noise.
All the prayers rising up to Us
    (shouted or mumbled)
are so much noise and very little
    substance—
    even less grace and mercy.
We'd like to address this to just the
prideful among you, but alas,
    there is great complicity
amongst all but the tiniest remnant.

It must be said that the professed
believer and absolute atheist
have a lot in common.
Throughout the day, We are invoked to
    damn someone or something.
    Usually someone.

Then, there are the warring powers
that claim Our fealty to their
    diabolical destruction.
We are, apparently, for the use and abuse
    of great democracies and autocrats,
of radical factions and orthodox adherents
who must prove they are right and
    possess all (of their so-called) truth.
Deception begins at home.

We know millions are sick and hurting.

    Sometimes self-inflicted.
    More often inflicted by others.
Your leaders seem to address each morning
with the same question over and over:
    What cruel thing can we do today?
How did they become your leaders?
    It wasn't our doing!

We get conflicting messages.
    Surely, you know that.
Some invoke a god of micromanagement—
the prayer only answered if on their terms.
    Others keep it vague.

Others still, though much less common,
seek poetic expression of their plight.
    Beautiful words
can bring comfort to the infirm
    of mind and body.
The prophets and mystics have known
of this power throughout the ages.
They have loved much and feared little.
    Sadly, the healing poetic words
fall on deaf ears where hubris and greed
    are the order of the day.

We are glad to laugh with you, and
We certainly weep with you and for you.
You have each other for comfort and strength.
This, and the beauty that surrounds you,
    are the greatest gifts.
    Their fruit is great joy.
These are your prayers answered.
    You need only knock on their door.
To do that, you must awaken.
We are the door, the portal.

The waking and the knocking
    are yours to do.

We have billions of galaxies to
    delight in;
a creation that is as amazing
as it is vast, and Earth stands out
    as a sphere as beautiful
as any perception of heaven itself.

Grow up! Instead of waiting for
our intervention, try owning the mess
you insist that We fix—or worse, that We
are blamed for through some twisted notion of
    divine authoritarianism.

You want free choice, and many of
you take it for yourselves and
do all to can to deny it to others.
    Don't invoke Our name
in your justification of such evil.

Some wonder how all
    the imperfections
of billions on billions of people
resolve to perfect love in the next life
when it is such a mess in the present.

When Job asked this, it is said
    we answered
    in vagaries
about his lack of presence when the
    foundations were laid.
That was the poet struggling for an
answer that never came. He figured,
when in doubt, state the obvious.

There are those, conveniently for others,
    never themselves,
who solve it by imagining an eternal torment
for the vast majority of you who have ever been.
They like unquenchable fire for others.

The universe wasn't built in a day or six.
You might have noticed with so much
going on, We seem to move
    at the speed of light one moment
    and as slow as a snail in the next.
We love the light for all it illumines,
but We love the snail, too, for its simple
existence in a diversity well beyond the
imagination of a few pounds of brain matter.
    Knowing this is true humility,
    as vital as it is rare amongst you.

You are the only creature on
    Our beloved Earth
that can destroy life in a cosmic zepto-second.
Stop sending your damnations and
pious platitudes Our direction.
Stop invoking Our name for your folly.

We really don't want to tune you out,
but you make it harder every Earthling day.
If you want your prayers to have effect,
    it's quite simple.
You might even find your awaited Heaven
    on Earth now.
That was the point we tried to make
    two Earthling millennia ago.
And before and since.

More love. Stop the hate.

More mercy. Stop the judgement.
More gratitude. Stop the damning.
More song. Stop the screaming.
    For your own sakes!
Yes, this is Our humble prayer for you.

The States of Mind and Soul

Hope and optimism seem to be
    interchangeable
in many people's minds.

It is not the same
with pessimism and despair.
Pessimists have far too much
confidence in their opinion
    to despair.

Are you optimistic or pessimistic
about the future? That seems about
as useful a question as, "Is your glass
    half full or half empty?"

(The politicians tell us perception is reality).

Neither of those questions ask anything
of us. All we need do is subscribe
    to a notion
of some future state.

Technology will save us.
Technology will destroy us.

Capitalism will save us.
Capitalism will destroy us.

Socialism will save us.
Socialism will destroy us.

Religion will save us.
Religion will destroy us.

No matter the view, the roots remain.
    If an optimist—blind devotion.
    If a pessimist—cynicism.
Both allow you to be glued to a status quo.
    Both are states of mind.

If you believe hope is our duty,
it must be acknowledged that
    despair lurks
    around every corner.

Hope requires us to trouble our minds
with all manner of complexities.
It demands that we resist despair, finding
    gratitude in simple things,
    beauty beyond the rubble,
    wholeness beyond the lies,
energy to press on in the present.

    Hope instills imagination.
It possesses great powers against despair.
These powers are free—kindness, generosity,
peaceableness, inclusion, compassion,
humility, forgiveness.
    Without these, hope dies.
Without hope, the soul dies.

This day, I shall feed my soul
    and live.

Elegy to Jack Corwin Graf (1947–2020)

It's not only miles that divided us.
Your life and mine were as different
    as night and day.
Your fidelity to place and kin were
real. Mine a construct of a wanderer
who never knew such a rooted presence.
Your life social, your place in community
active and enduring. Mine is better
described as that of a hermit wannabe.
Your life conventional—my life? Well,
conventional in a different fashion.
Our faith, which might have been
a common bond, was strained
    for too long
by a presumption of judgement
each held regarding the other
    (it must be said),
a dis-ease that infects too much
in too many families these days,
driven as we are by too many
to see duality in race and creed
    and kind.

Our mother, though a master of
staying connected to all her brood,
lacked the magical powers of keeping
that brood safely as one
    under her wing.
If this was a grief to her,
    as it surely might have been,
she never would have interposed
    herself forcefully
to try to change it. Like her father before
her, she let her children make their

own way in the world. Never hesitant
to point out anything she disapproved
of, but never enough to distance
    herself from that maternal love.
And never using one against another.

It is perhaps due to her, more than
any other, that across those miles
    and beyond the boundaries
    of our limited differences,
there resonated a frequency of care
and concern that could not pass
    from either of us.

(I never tried to let it pass.
Whether you tried or not, I cannot say).

If something good came from my
nomadic life, it was wandering back
into your life as that life approached
    its too painful end.
I couldn't change the pain or the past.
    None of us could.
But I was reminded why you always
held an enduring place of fondness in my heart. And
I know that death cannot steal that away.
    Rest well, big brother.

The Chasm

You judge me for who I love.
I judge you for who you hate.
For us to come together,
I must stop loving
    or you must stop hating.

    (Maybe it isn't hate.
It looks like it from over here).

My love is held with a simple vow
    and a life of fidelity.
Your right to your hate confirmed by
    tradition,
    orthodoxy,
a common conformity of purpose.
    This is your fidelity.

Odd that our fidelity stands as
such a hindrance between us.

Yet, the chasm isn't as wide
    as you might think.
My hand is here,
    reaching out,
if you ever want to reach across.

Finding Joy Beyond the Noise

I wish it were as easy as supporting
    a green new deal.
One windmill can take up to thirty thousand tons—
    sixty truckloads—of cement,
nine hundred tons of steel. Useful life expectancy?
Twenty to twenty-five years. Sound green?

(It $ure is green for the exploiters.)

Solar panels and batteries require
    mineral extraction of
lithium, cobalt, neodymium, terbium,
indium, dysprosium, and praseodymium—
    to name a few.
Most of these we've never heard of.
All of these require massive increases
    of current extraction
to meet anticipated demands.

(Carbon-neutral extraction, no doubt.)

    Plant-based diet advocates,
Who, as best I can tell, don't look at
the world around them, seem to think
we can feed the world and save the planet
if we only rid ourselves of animals
    in the food chain.
Never mind the resistance of grass to
pests, disease, cold, heat, flood, and draught.
    Never mind
the ruminant who can covert such
poor-quality food into vitamin- and
mineral-enriched protein and fat.
Never mind that holistic grazing practices

can reverse the fast-growing desertification
    across the globe.
Never mind the vulnerability of fruit and
vegetables to Mother Nature's torments
of early seasons, late seasons, wet seasons,
dry seasons, hail, wind, and fire.
    Never mind
the intensity of irrigation, low-paid labor to harvest,
and global transport non-native foods require
to get to market.
    Never mind the pace at which cities
cover over the small percentage of arable land
our celestial orb has given us.

Beware of anyone with the answers,
when what they propose is only
    as deep as
    their platitudes.
Beware of the politicians who
say they are all-in on a green new deal
while voting billions upon billions for
military spending, weapon exports,
    crippling sanctions,
    corporate bailouts.
Beware the religious who are against birth control
    but quick to support
    forever war.
Beware of the rock concert fundraisers
whose agenda conveniently offers
    more entertainment and
    self-righteous posturing
than thrift and conservation.

    Walk away
from the empty words, the empty
calories, the half-baked solutions.

    Walk away
from the billionaires and their minions
who assure us that technology will save us.
    Walk away
from your own complicity with
    extraction, pollution, trading
that keeps extracting the greatest
    toll on the poor.

    Support the farmer and rancher,
    as best you can,
who pasture their sheep, cattle, chickens, and
hogs in a more symbiotic relationship
    with all that is.
Stop your support of the disposable economy,
which includes stopping complicity with
the evil of seeing the other as disposable
    to secure your wealth and comfort.

Then, sit quietly with yourself and your world.
    Find joy beyond the noise.

The Inspiration of Dickens

His words transcend time,
    as truth always does.
Like that time in London and Paris.
    It is the best of times;
    it is the worst of times.
Times of wisdom and foolishness, too,
though the foolish seem
intent on drowning out the wise.
Thus it was and may well ever be.

    It is the worst of times.
Go online and you can
become a devotee of all
who lust for power.
    The glaring lie.
The art of the deal.
    They accumulate
for the sake of accumulation.
Others, just as foolish, divide, hate, instill fear.
While these folks think themselves clever,
    and somehow
more entitled to more than the rest of us,
the reality is a far cry,
summed up sufficiently in one word:
    nincompoopery.

    It is the best of times.
You can also go online and find
    music that inspires,
    poetry that nourishes,
a how-to video on anything imaginable,
    bloggers who devote their
humble cause to speaking truth,
even if their following is minuscule

and frequently attacked by
    the online haters
and commenters whose purpose
in life seems to be to defend stupidity,
regardless of the cost
    to their own soul and
    to the world.

My voice has grown weaker.
I can't make a joyful noise with the gusto
I once could. Maybe I'll get a cello.
My fingers still work,
    as does my hearing.
Perhaps the music within me
will find its next expression in the
tension of the bow on the strings.
Perhaps, too, the tension of the world
    against my mind
will find some expression
on a Sunday morning, to put down
the thoughts that still ramble
around the cluttered
    catacombs within.

I'll leave the nincompoops to their
sad existence—hell incarnate,
whether known or unknown.
They have nothing before them
in their season of darkness;
    the winter of despair
they have constructed.

To the healers, poets, musicians,
    gardeners, and simple folk—
we have everything before us
in our spring of hope.

Our season of light
shall not be extinguished.

April 2020

We can't find it.
It's out there somewhere.
    It must be.
Surely, it took a wrong turn and
is trying to find its way back to us.
Spring should have sprung by now.
    The news headline:
2020—set to be hottest year on record.
    April didn't get the memo.
She sent us another morning below freezing.
Ice crystals from the morning fog
on the frosty, uneven ground make
the old dog stumble as she tries to
    take care of her business.
She likes the cold more than we,
but even she has her limits, as the cold
morning makes for stiff legs and creaky hips.
She's eager to get back inside,
but her gait requires slow and steady.
    Buds on the trees
are holding off for a warmer day.
Dandelions thought they had the schedule
worked out, only to find that they were wrong.
A few made an early attempt, but
    they are sheltering in place again now.

It must be that the invisible virus has
infected our spring as it has our world.
It is cold and cruel, and it keeps us in isolation.
    It, too, shall pass,
but not soon enough for the lovers of spring.
    The lovers of life.
The lovers of blossom and flower and green.
We must accept the world as it is,

    not as we wish it to be.
Still, the promise remains.
The tree brings forth its fruit in due season.
    The due season
seems a bit confused at the moment.
She's in lockdown with the rest of us.
She's seen the death and forced solitude
of the grieving and seems afraid
of bringing forth new life too soon.
    Out of respect for the dead,
she withholds her rebirth for a time.
But the dead ask of her what they ask of us:
    Awaken and live!

Dark Hour of the Soul

I am estranged from the world.
    No, that is not right.
I am in love with this world.
There is beauty all around me.
The wild and tame creatures of this planet—
    fantastic.
The mountains, valleys, streams, and deserts—
    awe-inspiring.

Our little red heeler, Penny,
lived two kinds of lives:
one in which she was relaxed
and free among us, her pack,
and one of complete suspicion
and withdrawal from everyone else.
    Smart dog.
I think it's time to follow her lead.

    For it is my own species
from whom I am estranged.
The ugly words and even uglier deeds
that bombard us day after day.
The senseless violence and greed.
Destruction for profits' sake.
    Arrogance, hubris, pride.
People wrapped in the flag of
    blind nationalism.
Adherents to narrow, rigid beliefs
endlessly castigating others.
Lies, damn lies, and statistics.
    I'm weary of it all!
And I don't know a damn thing
    to do about it but retreat
for what remains of my days or years.

Deliver me from the great temptation to say,
    Farewell, friend and foe.
You shall not hear from me again.

Oh, powers of darkness! What are you doing
    to my hopeful soul?
Will you crush my life, as you have so many others?
Must I consign myself to your powers?
Your minions are many and boisterous—
    drowning out the voices
crying for freedom and dignity.
    Oh, powers of darkness!
One day, you might well usher in
a final Armageddon of destruction,
    invoking, unjustly—arrogantly—God's name.

    Get thee behind me!
Dark night, let loose my soul
that it may move again into the light
    of a world of beauty and grace.

In Closing

A Canticle for Peace
(Tune: Finlandia: verses 1–2 by Lloyd Stone, written at age 22, between WWI and WWII; verse 3 by Josh Mitteldorf; verse 4 adapted from the UU hymnal; verses 5–6 my own--my epitaph)

This is my song, oh God of all the nations,
a song of peace for lands afar and mine.
This is my home, the country where my heart is;
here are my hopes, my dreams, my holy shrine;
but other hearts in other lands are beating
with hopes and dreams as true and high as mine.

My country's skies are bluer than the ocean,
and sunlight beams on clover leaf and pine.
But other lands have sunlight, too, and clover,
and skies are everywhere as blue as mine.
This is my song, thou God of all the nations;
a song of peace for their land and for mine.

When nations rage, and fears erupt coercive,
the drumbeats sound, invoking pious cause.
My neighbors rise, their stalwart hearts they offer,
the gavels drop, suspending rights and laws.
While others wield their swords with blind devotion;
for peace I'll stand, my true and steadfast cause.

We would be one, as now we join in singing
our hymn of love, to pledge ourselves anew.
To that high cause of greater understanding
of who we are, and what in us is true.
We would be one in loving and forgiving,
with hopes and dreams as true and high as thine.

A dawn shall rise when peace prevails forever.
All wars have ceased, and tribal strife's no more.
I'll see anew, the beauty that surrounds us,
in humble thanks for all our world has given.
When in my heart all truth is gently beating,
my life's last breath is one with Thee, my Friend.

This is my end, and so my Just beginning.
I know not how my death shall bring new life.
What peace I've known, I've known was grace perfected,
as you, my Friend, have led me on my way.
Your mercy—great; your steadfast love has held me
and, thus, has healed me for the dawn of peace.

www.ingramcontent.com/pod-product-compliance
Lightning Source LLC
Chambersburg PA
CBHW051647040426
42446CB00009B/1022